Ref

THE TEACHERS
GUIDE TO
WORLD MUSIC

Conor Doherty & Richard Knight

**R. RHINEGOLD
EDUCATION**

www.rhinegoldeducation.co.uk

First publishued 2012 in Great Britain by
Rhinegold Education
14–15 Berners Street
London W1T 3LJ

www.rhinegoldeducation.co.uk

The Teacher's Guide to World Music
Order No. RHG416
ISBN: 978-1-907447-15-0

Exclusive Distributors:
Music Sales Limited
Distribution Centre, Newmarket Road
Bury St Edmunds, Suffolk, IP33 3YB, UK

Printed in the EU

CONTENTS

THE AUTHORS

Conor Doherty studied Music at University College Cork, with a particular focus on north Indian, west African, Javanese and traditional Irish music. After completing his BMus, Conor moved to Pakistan to study dhol drumming with the renowned Sufi dhol drummer Papu Sain. After three years he returned to London to complete a master's degree in ethnomusicology at Goldsmiths College.

In 2001, Conor began teaching ethnomusicology and music at The Brit School for Performing Arts in London. He has travelled extensively, taking lessons as he goes, including an extended period of study at the University of Ghana and gamelan lessons in Java. Conor is also a singer and guitarist, performing Irish and English folk music at clubs and festivals.

Richard Knight studied Music at St. John's College, Oxford, and has been Director of Music at two leading independent schools. He now combines teaching with a position as a senior examiner for one of the A-level exam boards, and is also on the examiner panel for the ABRSM. He has written several books for Rhinegold Education including study guides for GCSE, AS and A2 level. He is a keen traveller and has made extended trips to South America, having a particular interest in tango and Andean music. Richard is also a composer with a diverse range of works to his name, including opera, oratorio and chamber music.

COMPANION WEBSITE

The companion website hosts all of the online resources that accompany this book. It can be accessed by visiting **www.rhinegoldeducation.co.uk**, logging in to **My Rhinegold** and registering the book code **ZSNOPG**.

A PERSONAL ENCOUNTER

YASCAPI, BOLIVIA – AUGUST 2008

I am in a home that could hardly be more remote from my own: a mud-brick, single-storey abode that has as much accommodation – a room – for the family I have come to visit as it has space for the family's pigs. This is Demetrio's home: the 12-year-old Bolivian boy whom I sponsor. I have known Demetrio for three years through the photographs I have in my home back in England (courtesy of the charity acting as intermediary) and the letters and crayon drawings that I have received from him. Today is special: today I find myself in his home, with his mother and sister Norma.

The journey here has emphasised just how far apart we live. Not one, but four aeroplanes brought me from England to the old university city of Sucre, Bolivia. This morning Andrés, the charity's local man on the ground, met me in his jeep at my hotel and we have driven for some four hours to reach the hamlet of Yascapi, setting out before sunrise. The first hour was on a tarmac road; thereafter we were on rough tracks across an uncompromising landscape, passing through only one village along the way. Finally, on the wide, barren plateau of the altiplano, we spied the few roofs of Yascapi where approximately 200 people live. To my eyes, spoilt by first-world excess, it is not immediately apparent how. There is a beauty here: the purity of mountain-top air and lack of modern intrusions briefly tease the mind. The beauty does not make life here comfortable though; it does not hide the utter desolation. There are no mains utilities: Demetrio's daily routine starts with a walk before dawn to collect water for his family. The nights at this altitude are bitterly cold, and the climate not conducive to agriculture. Any entertainment, should life offer time for such trivialities, will have to be homespun.

Demetrio's home is not even in the main hamlet but out the other side by half a mile or so. Here I talk in my broken Spanish to him, and Andrés talks in Quechua to Demetrio's mother who has no Spanish. Remarkably we are treated to a cooked lunch, after which I try to teach Demetrio how to play with the frisbee I have taken with me: quite a challenge in the thin air that comes with being 4km above sea level. Andrés soon tells me that we should go back to the main hamlet and we all climb aboard his jeep, leaving Norma alone tending her pigs.

A little way down the track we are greeted by the women of Yascapi. They have dressed in their best – a local costume – and are waving white flags as part of a traditional dance. Where there is dancing there will be music. Sure enough Yascapi's local band is there: a group of four men. It becomes apparent that word of our visit preceded our arrival, and for the people of Yascapi, not used to seeing visitors (still less one with pale skin) that is reason enough to party. Parties are not so different continent to continent: music, dancing, laughter. I do as I am bidden: climb out of the jeep and join the dance.

These musicians are a remarkable quartet. They play homemade instruments, for where would they possibly go to buy them? One plays a large, booming drum, made from an old oil drum covered with a skin, most likely llama. This is strung over his shoulder. He beats it with a single crudely constructed beater: just the one because his other arm has been amputated above the elbow. His three fellow musicians play various types of pipe: variants of notched recorders, two straight and one curiously curved.

It occurs to me that there is a lot about this music-making that I should find appalling. All four men have been in the party mood for some time and copious amounts of the local brew – a maize beer called *chicha* – have been imbibed. Whether this is taking its toll is hard to say, but the drum beating is irregular both in rhythm and tone: the full-blooded hits boom, other more glancing blows provide unpredictable variations. Meanwhile, though it is apparent that the pipers are all intending to play the same melody over and over again, there appears to be failure to agree on exactly how it goes, no matter how many times it is played. Each of the three players fades out from time to time – perhaps even for them the lack of oxygen is a challenge when it comes to blowing a pipe – but after a moment they resume with renewed vigour, though not necessarily from the same point as the other musicians have reached. These three pipes can be really rather shrill when a new burst of energy seizes the player, and it is not readily apparent that all three share the same equal temperament when it comes to their tuning scale.

And here I am, a professional musician, who regularly examines live performance in schools and halls around Britain. What do I make of this extraordinary cacophonous din? A strange thing happens. Perhaps it is the altitude, or the spinning around in circles on the arm of a local lady in a dance whose steps are completely baffling to a novice, or the effects of increasing amounts of the, frankly, foul chicha that is frequently urged into my hand for immediate despatch: I have no time to analyse the situation. Whatever it is, I am starting to realise something. This music, for all its unrefined qualities, is true, genuine and joyous music-making. It is not music to be recorded and sold, or to be touted round the touristic hotspots of Latin America, or to be recreated in front of a ticket-buying audience. It is of the moment, of the place, of these people. It is being played to unite the residents of Yascapi on this unique day in their hamlet's history, to capture and express their excitement, to create the best atmosphere possible among the locals, and to honour their visitor: me.

No other music would convey all this here and now. A polished, meticulously prepared performance would not capture the moment or be shared by the locals as representing their world. These four musicians, inebriated though they are, are offering us a remarkable amount of themselves: the time they spent making their instruments, the way they treasure musical sounds that have accompanied them and their forbears in this remote landscape for generations, the warmth of their personalities in the fervour with which they play. All this they communicate through rather unpredictable thuds of the drum and squeals of the pipes where their Quechua mother tongue and my phrasebook Spanish fall short.

It dawns on me that little I have experienced in all my musical life has got me so close to the heart of the musical instinct in mankind.

This day was indeed a long journey: not just the four flights and hours bumping around inside Andrés' trusty jeep (it was most certainly worth the puncture on the way back that evening). It is the best part of four decades since my musical education started with a first piano lesson. Through school, university and my professional life I have pursued and held dear the great music of our Western world and its potential for profound utterance about the human condition. Now in my 40s, here I am in the remote, high Andes finding a new sense of wonder in a music that would seem to contradict much of my musical heritage and its values. There was no musical colossus of the stature of a Bach or a Beethoven in Yascapi today. Nonetheless, I have been deeply affected by the music I experienced.

Back in Sucre that evening, sitting in a bar, the sounds of the Yascapi band still circle inside my head. I resolve to return home and share my experience of this music with my students, and to explore the world's kaleidoscopic traditions of music with a more open and enquiring mind.

If only I had a book to help me and my students in our journey of exploration through this world of music...

Richard Knight, August 2012

INTRODUCTION

It is our hope that this book will provide you with a wide and varied range of material to use in your lessons, as well as the inspiration to develop your own knowledge and skills in this hugely diverse and, at times, daunting area of music-making.

This book is divided into two parts. The first deals with matters of theory and practice, ranging from defining what is meant by the term 'world music,' and why it matters in our schools, to how to go about creating successful world-music lessons and ensembles. The more extensive second part throws the spotlight on eight musical traditions in detail, providing material for learning, performing and composing.

Choosing the eight traditions to be included in this book was not easy, and some major areas of the world are unfortunately not represented here: China, eastern Europe and the Arab world for example. All of these areas have rich musical traditions that fully deserve engagement and exploration. For the purposes of this book, however, choices had to be made and we have picked eight styles that we believe work well in the classroom, and which provide a representative diversity of musical substance.

We have deliberately steered clear of proscribing each chapter or project to a particular age group. Much will depend on the demographic of your school, the resources and contact time you have at your disposal, and – importantly – your own enthusiasms. There is much here that will appeal to KS3 students, but some of the projects should also inspire your KS4 classes.

The book website

The second part of this book is supported by various supplementary resources – including a YouTube playlist for each chapter – that can be accessed from the book website at www.rhinegoldeducation.co.uk. Log in to 'My Rhinegold' and register the book code ZSNOPG to access these.

DEFINITIONS

WHAT DOES THE TERM 'WORLD MUSIC' MEAN?

Making music is, undoubtedly, one of the great human activities. It seems that wherever there is water there is life; wherever there is mankind there is music. We have made music in some unlikely places: the bushmen of the Kalahari Desert, the monks of Iona, the enslaved Africans on the cotton plantations and the prisoners at Auschwitz all created musical traditions.

So we have a whole world full of music, but the term 'world music' clearly isn't meant to encompass all of it. No one would include Western classical music under the 'world music' umbrella, for instance. What does the term actually mean, then?

The term is relatively new, and seems to have originated in American academic circles in the 1960s. It was taken up by the music industry in the 1980s, who wanted a convenient label for this new type of music that was becoming popular but couldn't easily be categorised. Thus in a large CD store, the term 'world music' has a similar significance to 'pop', 'jazz' and 'classical'. As the most recently added term to this list, it is generally used as a catch-all for any music that does not comfortably sit in any of the other categories.

At this level of classification each of these labels is obviously stretched to cover a bewildering array of musical styles, and the meaning of the actual word is taken to breaking point: thus Josquin de Pres, Mozart, Gustav Mahler and Pierre Boulez are all given the 'classical' label when one might argue that only one of them is truly a Classical composer. Similarly many a 'pop' musician might be insulted to be so-called, while there are plenty who desire to be popular but most definitely are not. Likewise, 'world music' can include a huge variety of musical styles from a vast number of places around the world.

So perhaps the easiest way to define 'world music' is to say what it is not: it is, very broadly speaking, not Western (i.e. European and American) classical, pop and jazz.

What does this leave? The following kinds of music can come under the banner:

1. **'Traditional' folk music**, which in the past has tended to share the following characteristics:

   * It is passed from generation to generation orally
   * It belongs to the 'folk' – traditionally the lower classes, rather than the upper classes
   * It often requires minimal musical training and can be performed by almost anyone, rather than just a few highly skilled musicians
   * It is usually by unknown or little-known composers.

   Examples include Celtic music, Eastern European gypsy music and Aboriginal music.

2. **Non-Western 'classical' music**. This differs from folk music in that it tends to consist of more complex, challenging music that is performed by specialist, virtuoso musicians. Examples include Japanese koto music (and the performer Kazue Sawai), West African kora music (Toumani Diabaté), and Indian classical music (Ravi Shankar).

3. **Non-Western 'popular' styles**, such as South African township music, Algerian raï and Brazilian samba.

4. **Modern fusion styles** that combine Western and non-Western elements. There are all sorts of manifestations of such new blends, for example:

   * Indian film composer Allah Rakha Rahman, who studied classical music at Trinity College of Music and combines Eastern classical and electronic sounds with traditional orchestral arrangements.
   * The kora player Mory Kanté from Guinea, who incorporates his traditional West African instrument into modern, pop-influenced contexts. His international hit song *Yé Ké Yé Ké* borrows rock, salsa and funk beats, and has been made into a dance remix by German techno duo Hardfloor.
   * Paris-based group Gotan Project, who integrate Argentine tango with electronic elements such as samples and beats.

Of course this list is rather oversimplified, and there are a huge number of crossovers and exceptions, but it should form a useful starting point. Nobody has managed to define exactly what should and shouldn't be labelled as 'world music'. Sometimes it depends not so much on the music but which country it is performed in, or who performs it. Consider these two performances:

* Rokia Traoré's recording of Gershwin's 'The Man I Love' on her 2008 album *Tchamantché*
* Simon & Garfunkel's version of the traditional Andean song 'El condor pasa' released in 1970.

The Mailian singer Rokia Traoré has taken a Western jazz standard and coloured it towards the end with her own African roots. Conversely, the American duo Simon & Garfunkel have taken a traditional Andean tune and turned it into a pop song, albeit one with a very Andean-sounding accompaniment. Are these examples of 'world music' or not? The ethnicity of the performers might sway you one way, and the sound of their music the other. You are likely to come across many pieces that could equally fit under the labels of 'jazz' or 'pop' as much as 'world music'.

ARE THERE DISADVANTAGES TO USING THE TERM 'WORLD MUSIC'?

Useful as it is to have terms that we can use to categorise the gigantic range of musical traditions and styles that assault our ears on an almost daily basis, there are dangers that labels such as 'classical', 'jazz', 'pop' and – perhaps above all – 'world music' pose.

By giving such a large body of music the same label, it is easy to assume that there is a strong similarity between all pieces that come under the umbrella term. This is clearly not the case, as any shortlist of world-music traditions would prove.

Here is a particular danger for music teachers. How many of us have heard the line 'classical music is so boring' from a student? Yet just how many of the constituent styles under this extremely stretched banner will that student have been exposed to before reciting this mantra with all the self-confidence of youth? With that one line a child can shut off to themselves, unknowingly, a corner of the 'cassical' repertoire with which they might identify or gain great pleasure. Moreover that corner might be the starting point for a lifelong growth of interest into many other places on the 'classical' map.

When we present world music we run a similar risk. How quickly will the impression formed by the first or second experience of music from the 'world music' stable become cemented as the opinion to be declaimed and promoted to friends as pertaining to all world music? Thus not responding positively to, say, Andean music might mean they approach gamelan with an already deeply rooted antipathy to it, and for no musical reason at all.

So take care how you use labels. As musically experienced adults, we have many pieces in place of the vast jigsaw that is the world's musical repertoire. To a child, who sees far less of the picture the jigsaw makes, labels can quickly become a shortcut to turning away from experiences they are yet to have and might well enjoy. It is much better for us to encourage a positive attitude to be receptive to all music on it its own terms, so that Machaut and Mahler, Gillespie and Goodman, The Beatles and Blur, gamelan and the balalaika are all met by open, enquiring minds.

One final disadvantage of the 'world music' label is that it can be used as a short-hand for music that we mean to keep at a distance. In other words, it can be used to accentuate the 'otherness' of music that will often be sung in a language we don't understand, and played on instruments that we are unused to. Labelling something as 'world music' automatically emphasises its 'exotic' nature (a connection which is actively encouraged by the music industry). At its worst, this can cause us to approach the music with suspicion and a somewhat condescending attitude – and by extent, this implies a similar approach to the people who make the music.

It is as though we are tempted to create a ghetto of 'world music'; though in our conceited first-world-centric view of music we fail to realise that we are actually creating a ghetto of our own musical tradition. There is a possibility that, as a result, our own music can either become fossilised (classical music) or formulaic and lacking in creative integrity through over-commercialisation (pop music). Engaging with other musical traditions refreshes our own musical instincts, in much the same way as we need to make new friends throughout our lives.

THE VALUE OF WORLD MUSIC

Professional classical musicians – players and teachers alike – enter their profession only after an exhaustive (and exhausting) training. There is no shortage of qualifications for the musician: the GCSE and A level, the grade examinations and diplomas, the degree and possible post-graduate study at a conservatoire, and for teachers the PGCE. Despite all this, it is not unusual to be a professional musician and yet still be a novice when it comes to world music.

With the resulting musical specialism that you may gain from such an intensive education, it can seem uncomfortable to meet another musical tradition for which you do not have an instinct. The temptation for all musicians can be to retreat to a more familiar territory: the instrument through which you daily express yourself, the repertoire with which you identify yourself. What, then, is to be gained from overcoming that initial discomfort, from letting go of your 'comfort blanket', and from setting out on an adventure into unknown musical lands?

World music as a window on the world

Wherever music has been created in the world (which is essentially anywhere and everywhere) it speaks of the people that have created it, the society in which they live and their experience of life. For the outsider to that society, music is a strong way to be drawn into the lives of other people.

For those who immerse themselves in classical music, this is something that can happen across time – a musical time-machine. The tourist to St. Mark's Basilica in Venice will immediately gather an impression of the opulence and lavishness of the society that built this unique cathedral; how much more vivid is the impression to hear the music of Gabrieli played in that building, the cornets and sackbuts echoing around the gilded cupolas.

In a similar way, world music can enable the receptive listener to travel the globe, from society to society, all from the comfort of a homely armchair. This really can be intercontinental travel without carbon emissions: world music lets us sample the lives of our fellow human beings all round the world.

World music as an entrée to foreign places

Embracing another person's music is a sure way to break down the barriers of distrust. These can arise with any new acquaintance: music is often not only a safe topic for discussion with strangers we may meet, but – unearthing a shared passion for Radiohead or Radio 3 – it can be a fast track to a new friendship. Much the same can occur when we arrive as a stranger in a different culture.

Many will know how learning just a few phrases of a foreign language can disproportionately enhance a visit to another country: locals are quick to warm to the tourist who has taken the trouble to learn their language. Some have a skill for languages, but many find anything more than a few words of a new tongue a mighty challenge. Music can provide an alternative way of connecting with local people. With just a little acclimatisation and an open mind, our musical skills can make this a more instinctive and, for the linguistically non-talented perhaps, enjoyable way to connect with people when we travel the world. If we are ready to embrace the music of a place we visit, we can soon join in; new friends will be made instantly.

World music as a way to cross social divides

The modern world does not only have borders between countries on a map. Today, communities of different ethnic origin are often found next to each other – this is almost certainly reflected in your school roll – and there is an all too clear potential for this to lead to social difficulties. Sharing musical traditions is a wonderful and enjoyable way to dilute these dangers.

If we engage with the music of the Jamaican family next door, or the large African community across town, we are likely to become not only familiar with some new music, but to learn about the costumes, festivals, dances and beliefs that go with that music. In short, we are likely to make new friends, forge stronger ties with local communities, and come to understand more about the people who live around us.

This is a particularly strong function of world music in schools: developing wider horizons – global horizons – in musical repertoire increases our students' sense of tolerance and openness to people of different backgrounds.

World music as a mirror on our own lives

World-music traditions are inspired by and rooted in a range of human experiences. Pieces reflect social traditions, religious practices, and life events such as birth, falling in love and death. In these ways, world music is not so different from the music of our own corner of the planet with which we are more familiar. World music can prove, therefore, the commonality of the human experience – however different life may look on the outside – and thereby undermine the temptation for those of us in the 'first' world to consider our experience of life somehow superior.

World music as a Global Positioning System for our place in the world

World music offers an instructive alternative approach to the performance, teaching and valuing of music. Music always reflects the values of the society that gives birth to it: Western music is dominated by famous individuals, composers and performers. World-music traditions are much more owned by communities.

Indeed, world music often conveys a strong sense of social cohesion: music may be created by a team of people, shared across generations, and celebrated by a whole village in dance or a fiesta. This contrasts markedly with most Western music, whether composed by a single revered master – a Bach or a Mahler – or created for commercial reasons in a more modern, popular style.

Consequently there is far less of a gap between musician and society in much world music than tends to exist in Western traditions. Music is played by musicians on behalf of a community and may be recreated afresh each time it is needed by that community. Moreover it can remind the musician not to be drawn into an egocentric approach to music-making – the *prima donna* tendency – but rather to seek to speak on behalf, as well as to, one's audience.

World music as a tool to enhance individual musical skills

There is a great pressure on aspiring musicians to become specialists. We choose a first-study instrument; we are drawn to particular areas of repertoire; we spend countless hours acquiring an expert technique. For the would-be orchestral musician or soloist, it is easy to be drawn into a vortex in which striving for expertise can reduce our musical horizons. World music can be an inspiring way to make sure that specialism is married to breadth.

The musical benefits of world music include:

* **Improved aural skills**. Most world music is learned and performed aurally, without notation. Learning music by ear is a very effective and efficient way of improving students' aural skills.
* **Improved ensemble skills**. Without notation (or a conductor) to rely on, you have to play while listening to what everyone else in the ensemble is doing and respond to that. An excellent example is playing gamelan: here one has to listen out for aural cues in the music in order to stay in time and to know where in the overall pattern of the piece you are at any given moment. In fact, in a gamelan ensemble it is common for everyone to switch places to learn each player's part. This enables you to hear the detail of the ensemble more clearly when you return to play your main part. Imagine how this would enhance the playing of a string quartet or wind quintet!
* **Better improvisation skills**. Many world-music traditions rely on some degree of improvisation, particularly as an embellishment to melodic ideas. This can be incorporated into practical activities in lessons.
* **Enhanced rhythmic skills**. A number of the more common world-music traditions found in schools – African drumming, samba, gamelan – tend to prioritise rhythm over melody and harmony. Ostinatos and riffs often have a strong rhythmic character. Getting the correct rhythmic groove is generally more important than the right pitch set. Performing such music improves rhythmic awareness which, in particular, can be a significant boost to students' composition work.

Above all, world music is participatory music: it invites us to relinquish our preconceptions – both of music and ourselves – and become fellow locals of musicians around the globe.

EXPLORING WORLD MUSIC

DECIDING WHERE TO START

Out of the many different geographical locations and musical styles covered by 'world music', how do you know with which one to start? As with all musical things, there is no 'one size fits all' correct answer, but certain styles are bound to suit you and your students better than others. The following advice should help you to narrow down your choice.

1. **Trust your own instincts.** Your own enthusiasm for a topic can make a real difference to how well it goes down among your students. With this in mind, the best place to start might just be with the music that – for whatever reason – you somehow feel drawn towards. 'Andean panpipes', 'African drumming' and 'East European gypsy music' probably all conjure up immediate pictures and sound worlds in your mind. Which do you most want to find out more about?

2. **Make use of your students.** Nothing beats the personal touch. It may well prove fruitful to find out whether any of your students have skills in world-music styles. Music often plays a vital role among ethnic minorities in helping to create a strong sense of identity and a link back to their 'homeland' (although be wary equally of assuming that a student from an ethnic minority will naturally have experience of a traditional music, and be willing to share it). In my own school we have, over the past few years, welcomed students who play the dhol, tabla, erhu and yangqin. They have given demonstrations in class and performances in school concerts.

   This has brought many benefits: the individuals concerned have gained confidence and increased their profile within their peer group; classes have been entranced by live performances on unfamiliar instruments by one of their own number revealing an artistic talent; and concert audiences (parents and colleagues) have found the unexpected diversity within a concert programme a very particular talking point. In short, the school as a whole has gained a more global flavour. Nothing brings down those false divides between musical styles quite as quickly as students playing their own world-music traditions.

3. **Think about the availability of resources.** You'll need some help to really get stuck into world music, and it's worth considering where you'll find it. For example:

   * Do you have a strong minority ethnic community in the local area, whose knowledge you can tap into?
   * Does a neighbouring school have its own steel band or samba group? Might they be able to loan their instruments (and teach you how to play them)?
   * Does your local music education hub own any instruments that you could make use of?
   * Are there any workshop providers nearby, and what do they specialise in?
   * Is it easy to find information on the style you've chosen?

4. **Start outside of music.** Consider using a current event, film or TV programme as a starting point and see where that takes you. For example:

   * A film such as *Slumdog Millionaire* (Indian music)
   * An event such as the 2016 Olympics from Rio de Janeiro (samba music)
   * A festival such as the Notting Hill Carnival (steel pans).

5. **Consider cross-curricular links.** Another possible catalyst for starting on a world-music topic might come from discussion with non-music department colleagues. World music makes for excellent cross-curricular projects. These might be at your suggestion, but could equally originate with another department's activity. Cultivating partnerships with colleagues in the geography department might be a good place to start. In addition, you may have colleagues with skills and experience from their own ethnic background who might be encouraged to share something of this with your students.

6. **Bear in mind your own background as a musician.** Your own musical strengths may give you a natural propensity for a particular style. For example, if you are a percussionist, or have a strong feel for rhythm, consider tackling a style that relies on complex rhythmic ostinatos (such as African drumming or Balinese gamelan).

7. **Think about whether you'd like to focus on a particular element or aspect of music.** If your aim is to spend a few lessons focusing on rhythm, then

samba drumming is likely to be a better bet than Indian classical music. Likewise, other styles will be better suited to illustrating different musical elements. A few more examples:

* Indian classical music is great for exploring scales and modes
* Rural Andean music can lead you into some interesting discussions on timbre
* A dance style – such as tango or salsa – is likely to be a good way of looking at melody and Western harmony, as such styles tend to have strong melodic lines and simple, repetitive chord progressions.

8. **Start with the more accessible styles first.** You may have a nagging feeling that when it comes to world music you've got to try to be as 'authentic' as possible, and hence assault your students with music that sounds alien and seems impenetrable, but this really doesn't have to be the case. Beginning with more accessible styles can be the best way to ease you and your students into world music. For example:

* Fusion styles, which incorporate elements of Western music, are a good place to start
* Music that has a strong rhythmic groove and/or relies on Western harmony is also likely to appeal to your students (such as African drumming or salsa)
* Gamelan, with its non-Western tunings and complex textures, can sometimes be a little harder to get into
* The same can be said for Indian classical music, with its long, meandering improvisations and lack of harmony.

9. **Decide if you want to buy instruments**, as if you do then there may be other considerations to take into account (see the section 'Getting practical' on page 24).

IDEAS FOR TEACHING WORLD MUSIC

One obvious challenge with world music is acquiring the knowledge to teach it; useful and clear information can sometimes be difficult to find. The second part of this book hopes to solve this problem by providing information, activities and ideas for eight different world-music styles. We will also try to point you in the right direction for other reliable resources.

You might perceive another challenge as being able to create an 'authentic' and 'meaningful' experience for your students, when you perhaps have no instruments, no in-depth knowledge, no grasp of the language, and are far removed from the original culture and setting of the music. However, the thorny issue of 'authenticity' is more down to a state of mind than anything concrete; in the chapter 'Issues in world music' on page 30 we will argue that the 'glass half full' approach is much more fun.

The third challenge might simply be getting your students interested in unfamiliar and strange music. Part of the answer to this is just finding the right sort of music, presenting it in the right way, and making it as relevant and accessible as possible.

To help you, a few general ideas and approaches are given below.

1. **Start with something practical.** It is much easier to get your head wrapped around strange, unfamiliar music if you spend a bit of time playing it. See the section below ('Getting practical') for more on this.

2. **Begin with more accessible music.** As mentioned above, certain styles will naturally be more appealing and accessible to your students. It is a good idea to start with these and then work outwards, to what might be considered the more 'traditional' or 'authentic' music of a country.

   A good rule of thumb here is to start with music in the cities and then move out to music in the countryside. For example, begin with highlife (a popular style that developed in the coastal towns of Ghana) and move on to traditional dance drumming.

3. **Use world music as one strand in a larger topic.** This is an easy way to start getting a bit more world music into your lessons. You can use it as one example when illustrating concepts or topics such as:

   * Syncopation (e.g. salsa)
   * Improvisation (e.g. Indian classical music)
   * Instrumental families, classified with the Hornbostel system (e.g. Andean panpipes for aerophones or the African balafon for idiophones)
   * Major and minor (e.g. tango)
   * Music for sporting events (e.g. Brazilian football songs).

This approach allows you to present world music alongside more familiar genres and styles; to tackle world music through a familiar concept or theme; and to emphasise some of the similarities between different cultures, rather than the differences.

You will find that in certain styles of world music the spotlight is often placed on one particular musical element, and this can make world music an excellent vehicle for exploring concepts such as rhythm, harmony, texture and timbre.

4. **Tie into a cross-curricular project.** One of the joys of teaching world music is that it's so easy to complement your work with that done by colleagues in other departments. There are many ways to do this and just a few examples are given below:

* **Geography**: an obvious link. Consider not just countries and continents but natural features such as rainforests (e.g. music from the Amazon basin) or mountains (e.g. Appalachian folksongs).
* **History**: many world-music traditions can be traced back through the centuries. For example, rural Andean music could be studied as part of a project on the Incas.
* **Religious Studies**: world music often has an important religious significance, particularly in India, Indonesia and the Middle East. For example, look at Balinese gamelan as part of the Hindu festival of Diwali.
* **DT**: world-music instruments can be fun if slightly time-consuming to make. A good place to start is with untuned percussion or Andean panpipes.
* **Art**: in the festival of Carnival (usually held at the start of Lent) the masks, costumes and floats can be just as important as the music, and so this event would make for an excellent collaboration with the art department.
* **Drama**: many world-music styles are linked to dance or drama. For example, you could team up with the drama department to devise and stage a shadow-puppet show accompanied by gamelan music.

5. **Make sure you explore the context.** It is much easier to get a grip on a world-music style if you can build up a picture of its context and setting. Learning about the beliefs, values and lifestyles of the people who make it is the best way to unlock the secrets behind why the music sounds like it does. It allows you to understand and enjoy the music to a far deeper level.

For example, the music of the Kaluli is very much influenced by their tropical rainforest home in Papua New Guinea. The layered, overlapping textures that sound out-of-time or out-of-synch with one another are a direct imitation of the rainforest soundscape. Studying the Kaluli's environment helps us to understand why their music can sound so unrhythmic.

When thinking about the context of the music, consider:

* The geographic location and the type of environment
* The social conditions of the people who make it – their class or social status and living conditions
* Other aspects of their culture – food, clothing, dance and art can all link into and have an affect on the music
* Any religious significance that the music has
* The type of venues the music is performed in
* Whether the music is in some way linked to a seasonal calendar, and performed for particular occasions and festivals
* If the music has a strong social function (i.e. is important in establishing a community's identity).

6. **Look at music in the UK.** There are numerous professional 'world music' musicians based in the UK. Likewise, there are many ethnic minority communities where music plays a huge part in their sense of identity. Music doesn't have to come from a far-flung place to qualify as 'world music', and studying music closer to home can make it seem more accessible.

7. **Look at music performed by young people.** There is sometimes a tendency to think that world music = venerable old men, perhaps sitting with their sitars (for example Ravi Shankar) or playing old-school Cuban music (cue the Buena Vista Social Club). Of course this is far from the case, and studying music that is created, performed or appropriated by young people can remind you that world music is very much a living tradition which is relevant to all ages.

For example, there is a type of popular music in Peru called 'chicha'. A blend of cumbia, folk and rock, it arose in the 1960s among the lower classes who were migrating from the countryside to the cities (especially the capital Lima). In particular, chicha was used to express the youth's experience in the city slums of dislocation and discrimination.

8. **Persevere!** An important lesson to learn in life, and world music is a good place to start: the more you can get your head around a type of music, the more you'll find something to enjoy about it.

It is important to remember that everything of the 'familiar' in our lives was once 'unfamiliar'. Life is all about embracing change, having new experiences, making new friends; education is the tool through which we realise the importance of, and discover a delight in, exploring the unfamiliar.

As teachers we should always challenge prejudice, and we have the experience to know how best to do this: self-belief in what we stand for (music in all its wondrous styles), a positive attitude, enough discipline to stamp down on unreasonable and unreasoned cynicism, and a well-judged musical diet that mixes some of our students' preference for familiar music with other unfamiliar styles.

GETTING PRACTICAL

Many world-music styles offer excellent potential for **group practical work** in class. While classical music is difficult to use in this way unless the students concerned have good instrumental ability and notation skills, and pop music can be challenging to do in a way that matches young people's expectations of how professionally mastered recordings make pop music sound, world music can be very rewarding.

Some of the reasons why world music can lend itself so well to classroom performance are:

* Some traditions are based on **repeating rhythmic patterns**. The simpler ones of these can be quickly learned by ear and adapted for various untuned percussion instruments. Examples can be found in African music and certain Latin styles such as samba and rumba. The rhythmic foundations behind styles such as tango and salsa can also be distilled in this way.
* **Repeating melodic patterns** are also found in some traditions, and these can be memorised in a similar way. Gamelan offers much material of this kind. Short melodic figures also occur in styles such as merengue and salsa.
* A number of world-music styles embrace a **heterophonic** technique for playing the main melodic material. Precision is not always that essential!

✳ Certain traditions give you the opportunity to participate in ways that **do not require instrumental resources**, be it the singing of South African gospel music or the use of hand-clapping, which can be incorporated into styles as diverse as Celtic and Cuban music.

One of the main benefits of world music is how inclusive it can be. It is rarely necessary to grapple with notation, and many instruments are relatively easy to pick up and play straight away; world music can give students the chance to play together in a large group without having to spend months or years learning a particular instrument and rehearsing written parts.

Workshops

There are countless organisations around the UK who provide school workshops in a variety of world-music styles. Such providers are well worth considering if you want to get practical music-making into your world-music lessons. There is much that outside providers can bring into a classroom: the authority that an 'expert' carries, the natural enthusiasm they can distil, the exciting range of instruments they bring, and their in-depth knowledge of the music. Being able to interact with real musicians also helps to bridge the gap between distant countries and the students' own worlds.

Most workshop providers can be very flexible, catering for a whole range of levels and group sizes. Workshops might range from a demonstration on various instruments (helped by a few willing assistants) to whole-class participation. While one-off workshops are most common, some providers will be able to offer residencies and long-term projects, which allow students to develop their musical skills and build up a real sense of cohesion within an ensemble.

A quick online search should throw up providers in your local area, but online teaching forums and word of mouth can often prove more valuable. It is likely that you already discuss professional matters with colleagues from other schools: your choice of examination boards, good local venues for a concert, recommendations for instrumental tutors and so on. World music should be on this list. Keep your ear to the grapevine, and sooner or later you will hear about a good world-music workshop that someone else has experienced.

Instruments

You can teach and play many types of world music without needing to buy any instruments at all. With a bit of creativity, it is possible to find a way to make most styles work on classroom instruments. However, to really get stuck into world music it's worth acquiring some instruments.

The following is a basic guide that will help you to decide which instruments to buy, who to buy them from and how to start playing them.

Decide which instruments to buy

There is little point in trying to build up a hotchpotch collection of instruments from around the world, as in the long-run you just won't be able to do very much with them. You'll find it much more profitable to pick one particular style and go for it. This will allow you to:

* Build up a complete set of instruments that will cater for a whole class
* Strengthen your knowledge of one particular style
* Set up an extra-curricular ensemble, so you can get the most out of your new instruments and create a sustainable project.

The four styles that are currently the most popular in UK schools are:

1. **African drumming** (using drums called 'djembes')
2. **Brazilian samba**
3. **Caribbean steel pans**
4. **Javanese or Balinese gamelan.**

These four have proven to suit whole-class use, and they're styles for which there are plenty of instruments, resources and support available.

Aside from the pointers given above (in the section 'Deciding where to start'), you should also consider the following when choosing which instruments to buy:

1. **Your initial budget.** Costs can vary hugely and the size of your budget may end up dictating which style you do (or don't) go for. Generally speaking, you'll find that djembes and samba drums are cheaper to buy than gamelan or steel pans.

2. **What you want to get out of the instruments.** What do you want to use the instruments for? Will you get them out occasionally to use in a KS3 lesson, or is your aim to set up a thriving extra-curricular ensemble? Answering these questions will help to determine whether or not you want to put the effort (and money) into purchasing high-quality, durable instruments.

3. **The stature of your players.** This won't affect which style you go for so much as what size of instruments you decide to buy. It can be an important consideration for both djembes (which need to fit easily between the legs) and samba drums (which are usually held by hand or strung from the shoulder). It is possible to buy light-weight, smaller drums from some suppliers that are more suited to primary children.

4. **Any recurring costs**, such as tuning steel pans or replacing drum heads. Some instruments will require more looking after than others, and it is worth bearing this in mind as you make your initial purchase. For example, if a set of steel pans goes out of tune then you'll need to get in an experienced tuner who may cost a few hundred pounds or more; if the same happens with a gamelan pot gong, a common solution is simply to stick a pound coin with blue-tack to the inside of the pot.

5. **Your storage and rehearsal space.** This is obviously important to think about if you are limited on either front. For example, it is possible to buy sets of samba drums that can be stored inside one another and so take up less room, whereas it would be impossible to do this with a gamelan. Likewise, moving a gamelan requires quite a lot of heavy-lifting and so really you need to be able to store it in the same place that you play it.

6. **Versatility.** This is worth thinking about if your department budget is overstretched, and it would help to buy instruments that can be used in a number of different contexts and situations. For example, untuned percussion (such as djembes and samba drums) will prove to be more versatile in the classroom than a gamelan, with its non-Western tuning.

Find a reputable supplier

Once you've decided what instruments to go for, who should you buy them from? Unfortunately not all world-music suppliers are entirely knowledgeable or inscrutable; in a market where the majority of customers don't really know a great deal about what they're buying, it's pretty easy to sell poor-quality instruments and get away with it. The sad truth is that it's not impossible to end up buying instruments that don't produce the right sounds, can't be tuned properly, break easily, are uncomfortable to hold and play, or aren't ethically sourced.

Bearing this in mind, one of the best things you can do is to undertake some research before buying anything. Talk to some of the suppliers and organisations who specialise in world music for schools. If you want to test their knowledge of their own instruments, you can ask questions such as:

* What are your instruments made out of? (This can have a real effect on the sound quality and durability of the instruments; a reputable supplier will know the answer to this and will be able to explain, for example, why their samba drums are made of aluminium rather than steel, and what difference this makes.)
* Where are your instruments sourced from? (It isn't fair to say that instruments sourced from their country of origin will always be of better quality. But on the whole, this indicates that the people responsible for making the instruments actually know something about them.)
* Why are your instruments more expensive/cheaper than your competitor's? (It is always worth finding out why you're paying more – or less – than you would for a competing supplier.)
* Can you provide 'spare parts' and servicing? (If not, can they at least point you in the right direction? If they can't, what are you going to do when someone puts their foot through a drum head?)
* Exactly what instruments are contained in your 30-player class package? (Beware that such 'whole-class' packages are often bulked up with finger cymbals, shakers and tambourines.)

Another word of warning is that you tend to get what you pay for. Expensive instruments will be more expensive for a good reason: they'll have a better sound quality, or be more durable, or lighter, or less likely to go out of tune. That isn't to say that you necessarily *need* expensive instruments, but that it's worth understanding why you're paying a particular price.

Don't be afraid of not doing everything at once. You can build up a whole-class set of instruments over a number of years. For example, if you can start off by purchasing a few tamborins, agogos and shakers, you can use the drums from a drum kit to create a fairly decent samba sound.

Learn how to play!

To get the most out of your instruments once you've brought them, you need to put enough energy and time into your new project to make it sustainable. Eventually, you want to be able to teach your chosen style with confidence. With this in mind, it is recommended that you:

1. **Get a specialist in to start you off**. See the section above on workshops – many workshop providers will be happy to help you set up your own ensemble, perhaps by leading the first half-term of rehearsals. They can be a good source of tuition, advice and music.

2. **Invest some of your own time** in learning the style yourself. You could:

    * Join a local group. The advantage to this is that it should be free or at least cheap to attend; the disadvantage is that it may take you a number of months to acquire enough technique and knowledge to run your own ensemble.
    * Find a course aimed specifically at music teachers. Such courses may introduce a variety of instruments and pieces, explore teaching methods, discuss differentiation and provide resources and lesson plans. A number of workshop providers offer such training.

If you simply don't have the money or time for either of the above, you can still get started using the popular teach-yourself method: search YouTube for instructional videos and invest in a couple of tutor books or DVDs.

ISSUES IN WORLD MUSIC

We have tried to keep the majority of this book as practical as possible. This chapter, however, has a more theoretical slant, and explores a few of the main issues that are present in the study of world music today. Being aware of such issues and giving them a little bit of thought will help you to teach world music more sensitively and critically.

Ethnomusicology

The term 'ethnomusicology' was coined by the Dutch academic Jaap Kunst in the 1950s, and developed out of the 19th-century study of 'comparative musicology'. It is an academic discipline that traditionally refers to the study of music outside the West. However, recent trends have also led a number of academics to begin studying Western music from an anthropological perspective. As a result, the field today is better defined not by the types of music studied, but by the methods and approaches used to study it (of which fieldwork is an integral element). Ethnomusicology shares many similarities with anthropology: if anthropology is 'the study of people', then ethnomusicology is 'the study of people making music'.

Authenticity

'Authentic' is a word that tends to hold much more weight than it should when it comes to world music. For Western classical music, the common view is that an 'authentic' performance is one that comes as close as possible to what the composer intended. There is a definite benchmark to aim for: an 'authentic' performance of Bach, for example, will aim to use similar forces, instruments and performing techniques as those present at the start of the 18th century. Authenticity, then, is usually an attempt to go back in time to the original performances of a piece of music.

How is authenticity approached in world music? To a large extent, the idea of going back in time is also the overriding factor. 'Authentic' is often equated with 'traditional', and when we think of 'traditional' we tend to picture a remote village in the countryside, 'unpolluted' by Western influences, where the older generations perform music that hasn't changed for decades or even centuries.

This view of authenticity is remarkably common, having been widely promulgated over the past couple of decades by the music industry in its attempt to market world music as a consumer product.

However, if we stop to think about this viewpoint for a moment, it starts to make very little sense. World music traditions are constantly evolving and changing: each musician that comes along can contribute something new to a style and help to develop it further. Ownership of most world-music styles – or even individual pieces – is not nearly as clear-cut as it is in Western classical music.

Given this, how is it possible for anyone to point their finger to a particular moment in the history of a world-music tradition and grandly claim that this was the pinnacle of 'authenticity', and hence everything that came before or after is, by definition, 'inauthentic'? Why is one musician inherently more 'authentic' than the next, and who gets to decide?

Perhaps the absurdity of this wouldn't really matter if it weren't for the fact that such a view of authenticity can have a very real, negative affect on the people who make the music. Musicians feel that they have to fit this mould to sell their music, even though they might not want to. In saying that we want our world music to remain 'pure' and 'authentic', we are essentially saying that we don't want our world musicians to become part of the developed world. As difficult as it can feel to know that musics, cultures and languages may be lost as a result, people have to be allowed to 'develop' all aspects of their lives as they wish. We also have to realise that no music is intrinsically better (or more 'authentic') than any other.

Another good reason for giving up on this rather narrow definition of authenticity is that your students will never be able to achieve it: they will never be able to recreate exactly a musical experience from another culture in their own classroom.

However, this is just as true of Baroque music as it is of world music, and should never form a barrier to teaching (and enjoying) world music. The study of another culture's music can provide such a wealth of knowledge, understanding and skills that the issue of being 'authentic' should fade into insignificance in the classroom. Remember, there are musicians all the over the world who are playing and studying Western music in their own way and getting much out of it. Their performances and understanding we may find unusual (or 'inauthentic'), but this shouldn't make their experiences any less worthy. We love to learn from each other and cultures over the centuries have been cross-fertilised by this very natural process. Of course in some situations (such as professional demonstrations) there is a need to get as close to the 'real thing' as possible, but this should never be an overriding concern for the school teacher.

Representation

Representation is a word that ethnomusicologists love. It is essentially a simple concept that deals with how you represent, depict and speak on behalf of other people. Of course it is important to represent anybody as truthfully and fairly as possible. But it is especially important when you speak for people who have difficulty making their own voice heard, which is why the concept of representation is so important in world music.

Therefore we might argue that, in the music classroom, it is more important to strive for accuracy than authenticity. For example, you could present to your students the 'authentic' recording of *El Condor Pasa* by the Andean group Intimani, and the 'inauthentic' version by the American duo Simon & Garfunkel, as two equally valid options: each has its place and one is not intrinsically better than the other. But it's important to make clear to your students what the cultural and musical context is for each of these songs, and to represent that context as accurately as you can.

On the one hand this is rather liberating, because once you realise authenticity is a dubious concept, you can ignore all of those nagging voices (perhaps including your own) that tell you world-music experiences always have to be as close to the original culture as possible.

On the other hand the issue of representation is important, and knowing what an accurate representation is can be near impossible when you know very little about the style of music you are teaching. The obvious advice here is to research a style of music as thoroughly as you can before you teach it. The chapters that follow in this book are intended to help you with this process. Other than that, you can only try to be as critical as possible. Rely as much as you can on information from people who have spent a good length of time in the culture that you are studying, and see page 34 for a few wrong assumptions that are commonly made about world music (including in textbooks!).

Ethnocentrism

Ethnocentrism is an important concept in ethnomusicology and one that's almost impossible to avoid. It basically refers to the idea that your own culture is 'central' and other cultures are consciously or unconsciously considered to have less value or importance. For the field of ethnomusicology this is inescapable to some extent: academics in other countries have to write in English if they want a platform for their work, most ethnomusicologists are from Western Europe or America and therefore naturally approach all musics from a Western perspective, and so on.

It is also impossible to avoid this in a classroom. But you *can* bear it in mind and try to approach a new type of world music as much as possible from an 'insider's' point of view: how would they conceptualise their music? How would they teach it? In what sort of contexts would they perform it? How do they feel about other cultures' musics?

This can lead into an excellent classroom discussion about the emic (from within the culture) and etic (from outside) views on something, challenging your students' perceptions of how they and other cultures view each other.

Comparative study

As mentioned earlier, ethnomusicology started out as 'comparative musicology'. It has always contained elements of comparison, although over the past few decades the arguments have become stronger for studying each music on its own terms, rather than making comparisons between them.

Naturally we always make comparisons with what we already know when faced with the unknown: when exploring new world musics, we compare them to other types of music that we are already familiar with. These comparisons are helpful when trying to get to grips with a new type of music. But at the same time, a music should be given the space to shine on its own terms. We should be wary of making comparisons that result in unfair opinions because we are judging something purely on our own one-sided terms, perhaps without entirely understanding the other side of the argument.

It is also worth noting that there is a danger in emphasising the differences between 'our' music and 'their' music. It contributes to our perception that people who make world music are 'weird', 'alien', 'exotic', and so on. At the same time, the differences are something that excite a lot of people about world music and you might as well take advantage of this fact. The best approach is to keep a balance: look out for the differences *and* the similarities but try to do so in as open a way as possible.

Common stereotypes

Below are a few of the most common stereotypes and generalisations that are made about world music, which you should try to avoid passing on to your students as much as possible.

1. World music is performed by tribes in small villages

Be wary of generalisations that promote a view that 'traditional' culture or beliefs are more widespread than they really are: that *all* generations or ethnic groups or social classes in any one place have the same 'traditional' views and ways of life. At its most drastic, such blanket generalisations can lead to a tendency to equate 'African music', as a typical example, with half-naked tribesmen dancing round fires in the middle of the bush. Such assumptions clearly neglect the huge diversity of situations, practices and beliefs that are held around the world, and contribute to the idea that world musicians aren't as 'developed' as their Western counterparts.

2. World music is ancient and unchanging

A characteristic example of this is the music industry's promotion of 'Incan' music from the Andes, despite the fact that the Incas were conquered and subjugated over four centuries ago. All music does change (although sometimes those changes are small or difficult for us to see), and the view that music remains 'static' is nonsense. Such a view also helps to promote the idea that people in other countries are somehow evolving more slowly than us.

3. World music is primitive

This links into the idea above. It is easy to view world music as 'simplistic' when judged against our own limited view of what is 'complex', and as a result we assume that the people who make world music must be 'simple' as well. In fact the world's musical traditions range from the very basic to the highly complex, and each fulfils its intended purpose and use.

4. People do world music all the time

Be wary of anyone who suggests that music is a part of 'everyday life' for an entire group of people, country or even continent. It is likely to be a sweeping generalisation that helps to promote the idea below.

5. This reflects their happy lifestyle

There is a tendency in the West to romanticise the simple 'peasant' lifestyle. The film *Avatar*, for example, does this wonderfully. Such a view often neglects the truth, which is that life as a subsistence farmer can be incredibly hard with little in the way of prospects, bad health, a lack of education and complete reliance upon unpredictable weather. Romanticising such a lifestyle allows us to ignore its problems more easily, removing any obligation we might feel to help people achieve something more. It also makes it easier for us to dismiss those who live this 'simple' lifestyle as being 'simple' themselves: either they don't know any better, or they don't want anything better, when the opposite is often much closer to the truth.

If you are interested in reading more about the issues and concepts involved in ethnomusicology, *The Study of Ethnomusicology: thirty-one issues and concepts* by Bruno Nettl is a brilliant, easy-to-read introduction to the field.

ANDEAN MUSIC

WHY TEACH ANDEAN MUSIC?

Few musical styles convey a landscape quite as evocatively as Andean music. This is a music that transports the listener to the vertiginous slopes and thin air of the great mountain chain of South America, where the condor rises on thermals high above grazing llamas and alpacas.

It is music that harks back to the Inca Empire, which flourished in the 15th century until it stretched the length of the Andes, reaching as far north as Colombia and down south into Chile. When the Spanish arrived in 1532, this remarkable culture was in many ways subjugated, and traditional pagan beliefs were renounced in favour of Catholicism. But although the Christian conquistadors even brought their own musicians with them (figures such as Juan de Araujo and Domenico Zipoli), traditional music did not die away. Andean music can, therefore, not only diminish the distance between your classroom and a different continent, it can also help to close the distance between the past and present, acting as a history lesson on one of the most famous (and earliest) civilisations in the world.

Andean music is a great participatory tradition. In the countryside, music is very much a community activity that everyone can join in with. Rural melodies are usually simple and repetitive – your students should find them easy to play – but they are also lively and full of energy. In fact, a refined playing technique is frequently eschewed in favour of an exuberant, energetic performance!

There are other reasons why Andean music is worth exploring:

* This is a great style for learning to spot and use: relative major and minor keys in quick succession; the effect of doubling melodic lines in parallel 3rds, 4ths or 5ths; and pentatonic melodies.
* Peru is one of the most popular gap-year destinations for students – the music can be both an introduction to the culture there and a pull for those with itchy feet!
* There is a real distinction between music in the cities and music in the countryside, which can lead to an interesting exploration of social class and cultural norms.

A BRIEF HISTORY

The rise of the Incas

Historical records of the Inca Empire are sparse; they did not have any written form of language (relying instead on an intriguing system of knotted rope called *quipu*), so we are dependent on archaeology and the accounts of the Spanish invaders for information. In the **11th century**, the Incas were a small tribe living in the area of modern-day Cusco (Peru). The first Sapa Inca ('Great Inca' or ruler) was **Manco Cápac**, who is thought to have ruled for some forty years at the very start of the 11th century. According to myth he was the son of the sun god Inti.

Expansion of the Inca Empire occurred in earnest under the ninth ruler, **Pachacuti**, who is thought to have ruled from 1438–71. Archaeologists believe that Machu Picchu was built in Pachacuti's reign. His son, Túpac, conquered their only rival for Andean dominance: the empire of Chimor further north in Peru. By the time that Pachacuti's grandson, **Huayna Capac**, came to power (c. 1493–1527), the Inca Empire stretched northwards to include most of Ecuador and even parts of Colombia; in the south, Inca territory included much of the north-west of Argentina and half of Chile.

The Spanish era

Following Huayna Capac's death, the Inca Empire suffered a **civil war** between two rival sons: Huáscar and Atahualpa. The Spanish conquistadors arrived into this unstable environment under the leadership of **Francisco Pizarro** in **1532**. Although they only numbered 168 men, their arms were superior and their tactics ruthless. Taking Atahualpa hostage after a surprise attack on the Incas, they extracted two rooms full of gold and silver as a ransom, and then killed him anyway.

The Spanish had one other unseen advantage: disease. The Inca Empire at its height had a population of several million, far more than half of whom succumbed to European diseases, smallpox especially. They had no immunity.

Once the Incan lands were conquered, the Spanish set about stripping them of their wealth. Above all they systematically ransacked the silver mine at Potosí (Bolivia) to which every indigenous family was required to send a son; the brutal working conditions meant that very few left the mines alive.

Spanish colonial domination lasted nearly **300 years**. Finally, weakened at home in the struggle against Napoleon, the Spanish crown yielded to uprising throughout its South American territories. Paraguay was the first to gain independence in 1811; Peru followed in 1821 and, finally, the much-exploited Bolivia gained its freedom in 1825.

The Andes today

For the Andes, the last two centuries have rarely been stable or prosperous. Frequent political strife has kept many in poverty. Development in the towns and cities has been slow to spread to the villages in the countryside, and as a consequence there is a noticeable divide between life in the city and life in the country.

Music in the countryside

Today in Peru and especially in Bolivia, descendents of the Incas – indigenous peasants known as **campesinos** – continue to live in a way that embraces many traditional aspects of their ancestors' lifestyles. Many only speak an indigenous language such as Quechua or Aymara, rather than Spanish. Agriculture on ancient terraces, irrigated by Incan water channels, continues in the valleys. Llamas and alpacas are still used to transport produce. Many villages have minimal or no electricity, with the community living in small adobe huts.

Festivals and celebrations form a focal point of a village's annual cycle, often blending Catholic teaching with older traditional beliefs. Music, too, is centred around these festivals and rarely heard outside of them. The festivals help to mark the passage of the year and music contributes to this with its seasonal nature – in many villages, different instruments and melodies are played at different times of the year. Music is traditionally considered to influence the weather: for example, tarkas are played to attract the rain during the wet season, and sikus are played to call a frost during the dry season.

Music in the countryside is frequently raucous and lively, and full of energy. One of the reasons for this is that music is often used as an offering to the local gods and spirits: it is believed that the more energy you put into a performance, the more you'll get out from the gods in return.

For an introduction to music in the rural Andes, watch YouTube video 'Andean 1: rural music'.

Music in the city

Life in the cities is much more Westernised. Most people here are **mestizos** – people of mixed European and indigenous descent – who only speak Spanish. Traditional 'pagan' beliefs are shunned in favour of Catholicism. Much will strike the Western eye as familiar: skyscrapers, taxis, men in suits going about their business, and so on. Yet often the modern world's influence plays out in a curiously individual way: the top soft drink is Inca-kola!

Music in the cities blends traditional Andean music with modern Western influences. As an introduction to the urban Andean sound, watch YouTube video 'Andean 2: Bolivia', in which the Bolivian band Los Kjarkas perform a number simply called *Bolivia*.

Discuss with your students how the traditional meets the modern in this performance. On the one hand, there are the traditional instruments and dress used by the performers, and the parallel melodies they sing. On the other hand, there is the use of guitar and drum kit, the soloistic playing, the Western harmony, and the whole 'pop concert' flavour of the performance. Nonetheless, this is very different to the pop music of the West.

Los Kjarkas is probably the most famous of modern Andean bands. They were originally formed by three brothers from the Cochabamba district of Bolivia in 1965. They helped to pioneer a new, popular-sounding type of folk music that has since become the face of Andean music around the world, and as a result of their success they have toured Europe, the USA and Japan.

In the Andes, the distinct **social divide** between the middle and lower classes (the mestizos and campesinos) forms a central element of most people's identity. Even today there is consistent discrimination against campesinos and their way of life (which, if anything, intensified in Bolivia after Evo Morales' election in 2006).

This divide also applies to music, but bands such as Los Kjarkas have helped to narrow the gap by taking elements of traditional music and incorporating them into a more familiar, Westernised package. This appropriation of folk music was partly fuelled by the rise of nationalism in the 1960s, but also occurred as a result of a realisation that the global music industry is keen to sell 'indigenous' music to the rest of the world.

Music from the Bolivian lowlands

The South American countries of Colombia, Ecuador, Peru and Bolivia are unique in that they all straddle the Andes and the Amazon basin: two areas that are geographically and culturally very distinct from each other. It can be interesting to take a look at how music changes in these countries as the altitude drops.

For example, the Chiquitania region in the east of Bolivia has an extraordinary tradition of Renaissance church music, which Jesuit missionaries introduced in the 18th century. It is still being played to this day by the local people (see for example YouTube video 'Andean 3: Chiquitania 1').

The people of Chiquitania also have their own indigenous music that can be heard during fiestas – listen for example to YouTube videos 'Andean 4: Chiquitania 2' and 'Andean 5: Chiquitania 3'.

INSTRUMENTATION

In the Andes, some instruments are heard almost exclusively in the countryside and some only in the cities, while others have managed to breach the divide between the two. The most distinctive Andean instruments are introduced below.

Drums

The main drum used in the Andes – both in urban and rural music – is the large bass drum called the **bombo**. Traditionally this is made from a hollowed-out tree trunk, with the skin for its head coming from the native llama. It is hung from a strap over the shoulder and sits by the hip. In the countryside it is usually played with one stick to keep the beat; in the city it can be played more virtuosically (see for example YouTube video 'Andean 6: bombo').

Flutes

The airy yet pure sound of the **quena** is something that most people immediately identify with the Andes. It is a vertical flute made from bamboo or wood, similar in size to the recorder. Despite the fact that most people think of this as an 'indigenous' instrument, it is almost exclusively used in urban music.

YouTube video 'Andean 7: quena 1' explains how to play the instrument, while 'Andean 8: quena 2' demonstrates some of its abilities.

The **tarka** is a chunky, wooden flute that is also played vertically like the recorder. The instrument is tuned to a pentatonic scale. In the countryside, different sizes of the tarka are played together to create melodies that sound in parallel 4ths and 5ths.

The instrument is intentionally overblown on certain notes to create a harsh, beating sound that is rich in harmonics and overtones. This timbre is known as *tara* and has many positive connotations such as balance, vitality, energy and generosity. YouTube video 'Andean 9: tarka' demonstrates a tarka troupe performing in a festival.

The **pinkillo** (or pinkillu) is a traditional herdsman's flute made of bamboo, again played vertically. Like the tarka it is played almost exclusively in the countryside, by troupes of men who are accompanied by a side drum. See for example YouTube video 'Andean 10: pinkillo'.

Panpipes

Panpipes are the iconic Andean instrument. There are a number of different types played across the Andes, but the panpipes whose sound you will probably be most familiar with – and the ones most commonly used in urban music – are known as **siku** or **zampoñas**.

The bamboo pipes that make up this instrument are arranged in two rows (known as *arka* and *ira*) and tuned to a G major scale:

In urban contexts, both of these rows are played by one person (as demonstrated in YouTube video 'Andean 11: siku 1'). In rural music, the two rows are split between different people, so one person plays an instrument made up of the arka row and another an instrument made up of the ira row. This playing technique, which shares the notes of the melody between two different musicians, is known as hocketing. For an example, watch YouTube video 'Andean 12: siku 2'.

Another type of panpipe played exclusively in the countryside is the **jula jula**, which only has four pipes in the ira row and three in the arka. These are traditionally played by men travelling on foot to a tinku festival (see for example YouTube video 'Andean 13: jula jula'). This celebration is held in Bolivia each May, and has gained widespread notoriety due to the ritual fighting that forms the heart of the festival.

Like the tarka, most rural panpipes come in different sizes that are tuned a 4th or 5th apart, played together to create melodies that sound in parallel 4ths and 5ths. However, in south Peru a style of music has developed that uses sikus tuned in minor 3rds. The result is beautiful and can be heard in YouTube video 'Andean 14: siku 3'.

String instruments

String instruments were introduced to the Andes by the Spanish, but were soon taken up by the indigenous people. The **violin** and **harp** are two instruments that have become popular in certain areas and modified slightly to suit local tastes. For an example, listen to the piece 'Pasacalle' from the album *Familia Pillco (Violins from the Andes)*, which is based on this opening idea:

Notice how the main melody has a pentatonic flavour and a rising, typically Andean shape. As the melody lifts up, the opening E minor chord on the harp yields to its relative major tonic (G major) at bar 4. After this opening phrase is repeated, the answering phrase drops down the other side of the mountain and returns to E minor.

The **guitar** is a frequent member of any urban ensemble, and it is often paired with the **charango**. This is a small fretted lute with a high-pitched sound that is both brittle and sweet. The soundbox was traditionally made from the shell of an armadillo, but nowadays is usually made from wood.

In the countryside, the charango is traditionally strummed by the men to accompany the women's singing; in the city, it is usually played more virtuosically. YouTube video 'Andean 15: charango' is a performance by the renowned Peruvian charango player, Julio Benavente Diaz.

Voice

Of course singing occurs the world over, but it is worth just taking note of the singing tradition of the Andes. In the countryside, it is traditionally the women who sing, the preferred style being high-pitched and quite nasal. YouTube video 'Andean 16: voice' is a very typical Andean music video, with the solo singer accompanied by charango.

CHARACTERISTIC FEATURES OF THE STYLE

Music in the countryside

Rural music can vary from one village to the next, as it frequently plays an important role in establishing a community's unique identity. Having said that, there are common characteristics and much instrumental music in the rural Andes consists of the following:

* A monophonic melody
* Played by a large group of men, all on (different sizes of) the same instrument
* Which sounds in parallel 4ths and 5ths
* And is accompanied by a bombo to keep the beat.

The melody is usually:

* Repeated over and over with no variations
* Highly syncopated
* Pentatonic.

For an example, watch YouTube video 'Andean 17: rural music'.

Music in the city

The standard line-up for an urban Andean band is a quintet of musicians playing guitar, charango, quena, panpipes and bombo. Common characteristics of urban music include:

* A focus on soft, mellow timbres (such as the quena and lower-pitched panpipes).

* Long, arch-shaped melodies that soar upwards and then return to where they started.
* A preference for lively, rhythmic dance styles.
* The incorporation of a European harmonic palette. Harmony frequently switches between V⁷–I of a major key and V⁷–I of its relative minor; chord IV is also commonly used in the major passages.
* Scope for soloistic playing by individual musicians.
* A strumming pattern in the charango part of 'down – down/up' with one long stroke followed by two short strokes. This is typical of a style called **huayño** (see YouTube video 'Andean 18: huayno').

For an example of a typical urban piece, watch YouTube video 'Andean 19: urban music'.

LISTENING EXAMPLE

Hector Soto: Charango del sol

Soto is a much revered Chilean charango player, and this track from his album *Mis Mayores Exitos* (My Greatest Hits) is available to listen to on YouTube ('Andean 20: Charango del sol'). The main melody comes in four sections:

This piece starts with a striking yet characteristic introduction, with tremolo charango chords that support a descending chromatic line at the top. Two other features to listen for are:

* The huayño rhythm in the chords (strummed sometimes on charango and sometimes on guitar), with the telling long-short-short pattern.
* How much of the melody is doubled in 3rds when played by the charango.

The piece follows this structure:

Introduction	
0:00	Tremolo charango chords.
0:16	The tempo and huayño character is established.
Verse 1	
0:26	Section A: quena takes the tune; guitar enters with offbeat chords.
0:36	Section B: quena continues with the melody.
0:48	Section A: melody now played by the charango.
0:58	Section B: charango continues with the melody.
1:10	Section C: quena returns to take the melody for this section.
1:25	Section D: charango takes over the tune.
Interlude	
1:45	Similar to the introduction, but the chords are more rhythmic and note the additional descending scale in the bass guitar at 1:53.
Verse 2	
2:04	This verse follows the same structure and instrumentation as verse 1.
Coda	
3:24	This is also based on the introduction, finishing with the descending scale in the guitar.

There are also some harmonic aspects that you may like to highlight. Section A starts in G minor and cadences in B♭ major (the relative major); section B starts in B♭ major and cadences in G minor. This switch between the relative major and minor is a typically Andean characteristic. The full progression is:

Section A				Section B				
bar 1	bar 2	bar 3	bar 4	bar 5	bar 6	bar 7	bar 8	bar 9
Gm	E♭	F^7	B♭	B♭	B♭	B♭	D^7	Gm

In addition, listen for the short circle of 5ths progression at the start of section C (G^7, Cm, F^7, B♭).

Los Folkloristas: Adiós Pueblo de Ayacucho

Los Folkloristas is actually a Mexican group of seven musicians. Founded in 1966, they are dedicated to playing music from across Latin America. This song refers to the city of Ayacucho, which is the capital of the Huamanga province in southern Peru. The city was so named following the last major battle of the Peruvian War of Independence, in December 1824. The victorious Simón Bolívar named the city after the Quechuan words *aya* (death) and *kuchu* (corner).

This song is available from iTunes (on the album *Camino de los Andes*) and Spotify (on the album *Los Folkloristas: Perú*).

The song has two principal melodic phrases, of which the first is:

Here is another Andean melody that typically falls from a major opening to a minor conclusion.

The work follows this structure:

Introduction	
0:00	A low guitar line starts; charango and a violin melody enter at 0:06.
Verse 1	
0:16	Two female voices enter with phrase A, repeating it at 0:25. (Note the slides that decorate the melody, which are a typical feature of Andean singing. Note too the ascending scale in the guitar at 0:23 – a characteristic Andean fill to add a bit of interest between phrases.)

0:34	The singers continue with phrase B, which is repeated at 0:43. (Note that phrase B has a different beginning to phrase A but then ends the same: this is typical of Andean melodies.)
Instrumental verse	
0:53	Quena, with violin an octave lower, plays phrase A (and again at 1:02).
1:12	Quena and violin continue with phrase B twice (repeating at 1:19); the charango has a triplet strumming pattern.
1:27	The charango and guitar have a brief interlude.
Verse 2	
1:34	The singers return with phrase A, which is repeated at 1:43. Phrase B is first heard at 1:52 and repeated at 2:00.
Instrumental verse	
2:11	This time the charango takes the spotlight; phrase A is played twice, repeating at 2:19. Phrase B is first heard at 2:27 and repeated at 2:34. As before, a short interlude follows.
Verse 3	
2:48	The singers return with phrase A, which is repeated at 2:57. This time the quena plays with the voices. Phrase B is first heard at 3:06 and repeated at 3:14.
3:22	A new melody – phrase C – is introduced, which is also repeated at 3:29.
Coda	
3:36	Quena and charango come to the fore to repeat phrase C; a modal final cadence (Bm–Em) is heard at 3:49.

Two rural Bolivian pieces

The two pieces discussed below both come from the south-west of Bolivia near the Salar de Uyuni – the world's largest salt flat. This is a remote, barren and high altiplano region, where communities are small and life is hard. Most villagers eek out a living as subsistence farmers. The two pieces below demonstrate the type of rural music typically heard in this region.

Chillima	Dionisio López
YouTube video 'Andean 21: Chillima'	YouTube video 'Andean 22: Dionisio Lopez'
From the village of Tahua	From the village of Estancia Aguaquiza
North of the Salar de Uyuni	South of the Salar de Uyuni
Language: Quechua	Language: Aymara
Played on sikus	Played on tarkas ('anatas' in Aymara)
Played in the dry season, including at the festival of Virgin del Carmen (July 16th)	Played in the rainy season, including at Carnival just before Lent

Chillima

This piece is performed by a siku ensemble accompanied by bombos. Characteristic features include:

* The steady beat on the bombo (which is the instrument used to signal the start of the piece)
* A pentatonic and strongly syncopated melody, with an AABB phrase structure
* High-pitched, nasal singing that features slides between almost every note
* A sudden increase in tempo towards the end of the piece.

Dionisio López

This piece is performed on tarkas rather than sikus, but otherwise shares many similar features to *Chillima*. One of the most interesting aspects of this performance is the harsh, overblown sound that the performers are striving for (particularly on the long notes). As mentioned earlier on page 41, this sound is embodied by the concept of 'tara', which has positive connotations of balance, vitality, energy and generosity. The opposite of tara is *q'iwa*: this refers to a thin, clean, pure sound and has negative connotations of imbalance, loneliness, infertility and selfishness.

An exploration of tara and q'iwa can lead to interesting discussions about timbre, and the assumptions we make about what a pleasant or nice-sounding timbre is. What do your students think of the 'tara' sound? Can they suggest how this sound might embody the positive connotations mentioned above?

PERFORMING

We mentioned the Bolivian band Los Kjarkas earlier in this chapter. An arrangement of their hit number *Llorando se fue*, released in 1981, is available on the book website. You can find the piece on a number of different albums and there are also many performances on YouTube (see for example YouTube video 'Andean 23: Llorando se fue').

The score on the book website can be adapted in various ways, but you could:

* Aim for an ABA structure: instrumental – singing – instrumental
* Have flutes (ideally panpipes or recorders) or other melody instruments on the upper lines
* Allow guitarists and keyboard players to follow the chord symbols
* Allow bass guitarists and other bass instruments to play the bottom stave.

Note that Los Kjarkas perform this song a semitone lower, but the key of the score on the book website is more guitar-friendly.

Characteristic features of this piece include:

* The AABB structure where phrase A moves from E minor to its relative G major, and phrase B goes back to E minor.
* The harmonic rhythm of the opening, which creates a 3 + 3 + 2 rhythmic pattern that is a Latin American hallmark.
* The melody of phrase A is best doubled at the 3rd below, while phrase B needs to be doubled at the 6th below.

Discussion point

This song has an unusual and interesting history:

* It was released in 1981 by a traditional Bolivian band.
* In 1985, Cuarteto Continental from Peru recorded an upbeat version of the song, featuring a prominent accordion part and more of a beat. (See YouTube video 'Andean 24: Cuarteto Continental'.)
* In 1989, the French pop group Kaoma, along with Brazilian singer Loalwa Braz, released a version sung in Portuguese called *Lambada*. It was top of the French charts for 12 weeks and reached No. 4 in the UK charts,

starting a lambada dance craze. It was, however, an unauthorised copy of the Los Kjarkas original, and in 1990 the Bolivian band won a lawsuit against Kaoma's producer. (See YouTube video 'Andean 25: Kaoma'.)

* In 2011, Jennifer Lopez released her song *On the Floor* – an up-tempo pop song featuring the Amercian rapper Pitbull, which also samples the *Llorando se fue* melody. (See YouTube video 'Andean 26: Lopez'.)

There is much to discuss here that reflects on the globalisation of world music. In particular, you might like to ask your students:

* Is it ethical to re-arrange someone else's work rather than writing your own? And without their permission?
* Does it make any difference if the arranger is from the same/different ethnic background?
* What role does the legal profession play in the arts?
* Why should Jennifer Lopez be drawn to use a Bolivian tune in her music?
* What does it say about the world in 2011 that a tune by a Bolivian band should be fused with an American rapper by a singer of Puerto Rican descent?
* Which is the more incongruous addition to an Andean line-up: an accordion, a rapper, or an international film and fashion star?

COMPOSING

In Andean music, the focus is very much on the melodic content. Melodies tend to be short, and they are often structured in two complementary phrases with repetitive elements. As a result, Andean music can make an excellent project for inexperienced composers.

The intention for this project is to write an Andean-sounding flute melody that reflects various aspects of the tradition, and a guitar or keyboard accompaniment to go with it.

Notation might be helpful, but – in keeping with Andean ways – this might well be a good composing project to undertake aurally, improvising melodic ideas and making sure they are catchy enough to be memorable!

Step one: composing section A

Section A should be 4–8 bars long, starting on an E minor chord and finishing on a G major chord. Your students should work out the guitar/keyboard chords first, perhaps using the long–short–short strumming pattern of the huayño, and following this line as a guide:

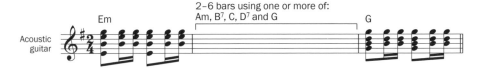

Once your students have decided on the chord pattern, they can work on the melody. They may like to use the full diatonic range of notes (i.e. the notes of a G major scale), or – to make it a little simpler to compose – you could restrict their options to a pentatonic scale using the notes E, G, A, B and D.

As a general rule, the first note in each bar should be one of the notes of the chord at that point. It is also a good stylistic trick to repeat small patterns of notes. Finally, your students should aim for some syncopated patterns. We have seen and heard a lot of the semiquaver + quaver + semiquaver pattern in this chapter; you might want to encourage your students to use it in their compositions.

Your students might arrive at something like this:

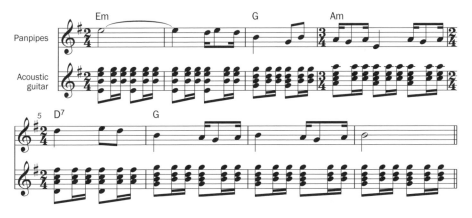

Step two: composing section B

Section B can be composed in much the same way. It should be a similar length to section A, although it doesn't need to have an identical number of bars. It is probably best to start this section with a major chord (G, C or D) and move (perhaps via B⁷) back to E minor by the end.

Your students might like to use the following line as a prompt:

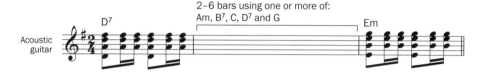

Step three: finishing touches

Other things your students could add include:

* An introduction: how about a short melodic phrase on the guitar before it then establishes the strumming pattern prior to the entry of the melody?
* Offbeat chords on a second guitar (or better still, give the huayño strumming pattern to a charango and have the guitar playing only on the offbeats).
* Some doubling of the melody at the 3rd or 6th.
* A part for percussion (such as a bombo line).
* A final flourish to round off the piece.

An example piece that follows the rules above is provided on the book website.

CROSS-CURRICULAR LINKS

Art link: in terms of visual art, the Andeans are probably best known for their colourful textiles. Many communities in the Andes have a strong tradition of weaving; the textiles of the Jalq'a in Bolivia are perhaps one of the most intriguing and impressive examples to start with.

History link: the Incas are the obvious topic of study here and can provide a wealth of material. There are numerous aspects of their remarkable society that are worth studying, including architecture (and Machu Picchu), agriculture (and terrace farming), and their system of communicating with knotted lengths of rope.

Geography link: the Bolivian altiplano is perhaps the most interesting area of the Andes to study in terms of its geography. It encompasses the world's largest salt flat and highest navigable lake, and is not far from the world's driest desert as well.

Citizenship/PSHE link: the humble coca plant has a hugely important role in traditional Andean society. It is used in offerings, drunk as tea, chewed when working and it provides a vital source of income for many families who grow the plant. It is, however, also used to manufacture cocaine, which has led to a long-running feud between Bolivia and America over the legality of its growth. Your students could investigate this argument further: do they think Bolivians should be left in peace to grow and consume coca, or is the only way to crack down on cocaine to prevent the growth of coca?

RESOURCES

Andean music hasn't infiltrated the UK (and UK schools) in the same way that most of the other styles in the book have, and as a result there are limited resources available to support your teaching of it. The following, however, may prove useful:

* **Book**: *Music in the Andes* by Thomas Turino (Oxford University Press, 2008) – a short book that provides a good introduction to Andean music, accompanied by a CD.
* **Workshops**: the organisation Musiko Musika (www.musikomusika.org) provides school workshops on Andean and Latin American music.
* **CDs**: any of Los Kjarkas' albums will provide a good introduction to urban Andean music. An excellent CD of rural Andean music is *Mountain Music of Peru, Vol. 2* (Smithsonian Folkways).

CALYPSO

WHY TEACH CALYPSO?

Calypso is the sound that accompanies the Caribbean stereotype of white sand, turquoise sea, palm trees, sun, smiles and cocktails. Of course it is a style that should find an enthusiastic response if you have a large Caribbean community in your school, and it can be a great opportunity for these children to express themselves and take a lead in their class. It is, however, a style whose appeal can also stretch much further.

Steel pans are the instrument most associated with the calypso sound, and a testament to man's instinct for creating music from the most unlikely apparatus. Steel pans are a resource well worth thinking about investing in. They do take up quite a bit of space (and their sound is curiously penetrative), but they are accessible to all. The technique is not complicated: no tricky embouchure, no awkward fingering, no challenging bow hold, no need for a trained musical ear to aid pitching. As such they are a fabulous medium for all to experience the collective creativity of ensemble music-making.

Watch a group of children perform a piece on steel pans and an infectious sense of joy very quickly builds up between the players and passes to the audience. Calypso music is lively and upbeat, and not a difficult style to comprehend or appreciate. Other reasons why you might like to teach calypso include:

* Sung calypso frequently acts as a form of social and political commentary, and this extra dimension can help you and your students to explore interesting topical issues.
* In Trinidad, the genre is taken as seriously by children as adults, with an active youth scene (as demonstrated by the Junior Panorama and Junior Calypso Monarch competitions).
* The development of calypso is intrinsically linked to the slave trade, making it a good style through which to investigate African slavery.
* It could lead to a great songwriting project.

A BRIEF HISTORY

Discovery of the Caribbean

The Caribbean is first and foremost a tropical sea, east of Central America and north of South America. The west of this sea is lined by more than **7,000 islands** that range in size from Cuba in the west, to the smaller islands and tiny islets collectively known as the Lesser Antilles in the east.

Calypso originated in **Trinidad and Tobago** – two neighbouring islands that are together known as one country, situated at the south end of the Lesser Antilles. Trinidad is the fifth largest island in the Caribbean and also the most southerly, sitting at just 7 miles off the coast of Venezuela.

Christopher Columbus 'discovered' the Caribbean at the end of the 15th century. Having greatly underestimated the size of the earth, he thought he was finding a short route to India; hence why, when his error became clear, the lands he found became known as the **West Indies**. His first sighting of land (somewhere in the modern-day Bahamas) occurred on 12th October 1492, and he spent the next decade exploring the region, returning to his native Spain from time to time to report to his royal patrons, take back treasures, and collect further soldiers and would-be colonists.

The name 'Caribbean' comes from one of the native tribes that Columbus encountered: the **Carib**. These people originated from Venezuela, moving north to usurp the place of other tribes (principally the Arawaks) in the Lesser Antilles around AD 1200, gaining a reputation for being fearsome warriors. They were decimated by the arrival of the Europeans, either through war or disease, and their identity was further diluted by interbreeding and assimilation.

The colonial period

After the voyages of Columbus, the Caribbean region became a competitive arena for European powers to explore, colonise and exploit. Major players in this battle for influence were the Spanish, French, Dutch and British.

The prime motivation for these European nations, beyond the obvious matter of pure power, was trade. While the Spaniards in South America chased precious metals (see page 37), the main trade in the Caribbean was **sugar**.

Transformation of the Caribbean islands was rapid. Barbados, for example, was largely unoccupied at the start of the 17th century. The first sugar cane was planted in 1637, and by 1660 the island had a population of 40,000, nearly all due to sugar. There was, however, a very dark side to all of this activity: **slavery**.

Slaves were needed to work on the sugar plantations and this led to a highly profitable, **triangular trading system** between the Caribbean, Europe and West Africa: African slaves were shipped to the Caribbean to work on the plantations; the crops they grew were exported to Europe; European goods were transported to Africa and used to buy more slaves.

The scale of this soon became astronomical: during the 18th century, it is estimated that Europe imported some 12 million tons of sugar at the cost of millions of slave lives (many not even surviving the journey across the Atlantic in appalling conditions). Half of all civil and naval shipping in this era was concerned with running and protecting the sugar and slave businesses.

This was largely the story of Trinidad's colonial period. The Spanish settled on this island in 1592. They opened up the island to immigration in 1776, in an attempt to make it more profitable, and during the next two decades many French migrated to Trinidad from other islands in the Caribbean, bringing their African slaves with them. These slaves, of course, were set to work on the sugar plantations and sugar quickly became the main export of the island. Trinidad was taken over by the British in 1797, who ruled until the island gained independence.

Due to the tenacious campaigning of **William Wilberforce**, the British slave trade was abolished in 1807, and slavery itself in 1833. Other European countries likewise abolished slavery in their colonies during the first half of the 19th century (although Spain was slow to act on slavery in Cuba and Puerto Rico, which continued until the 1870s).

After the slave trade

To prevent the sugar plantations from collapsing after the abolition of slavery, many landowners came up with a new scheme: to import **indentured labourers** to take the place of the African slaves. A landowner would pay for a worker's passage and provide them with food, shelter and clothing for the length of their servitude (usually around five years). In Trinidad and Tobago, this practice led to an influx of **Indian** immigrants in particular, which is why the official 2000 census lists the two main ethnic groups as being Indian and African. The descendants of the slaves and indentured servants make up roughly 80% of today's population on the island.

The decline of the sugar industry around the turn of the 20th century – which was largely down to competition from European beet sugar – led to widespread poverty, unemployment and a spate of riots throughout the Caribbean. This in turn helped a number of islands to gain **independence** from the 1960s onwards (including Trinidad and Tobago in 1962).

Although other exports were developed to prop up the Caribbean's economy – such as bananas in Jamaica and petroleum in Trinidad – few islands have achieved self-sufficiency and many are still suffering from the after-effects of the declining sugar industry. A number of the smaller islands now depend almost entirely on the growing tourist trade, which can be seen to have had both positive and negative impacts on the Caribbean.

CALYPSO AND STEEL BANDS

Canboulay

Like so much of Caribbean music, the roots of calypso lie in Africa, and in particular a work song called the *gayup*, which the slaves brought with them from their homeland. The gayup featured a lead singer called the *chantwell*, and a call-and-response structure.

Gayup songs were used on the plantations to motivate the workers, but they were also adapted for the slaves' Carnival festivities. As they were prohibited from taking part in the European celebrations (consisting of masked balls and street parades), the slaves developed their own festival known as **Canboulay**. This word is a distortion of the French *cannes bruleé*, meaning 'burnt canes', referring to the activity of burning the sugar-cane fields after they had been harvested.

Stick fighting was a central element of the Canboulay celebrations. This was accompanied by drumming and a type of singing called *kalinda*, which developed out of the gayup work songs and formed an antecedent to calypso. Each band of stick fighters would be accompanied by their own chantwell, who would use song to boast about their own band while belittling their opponent's. The sharp and satirical nature of these songs became one of the defining features of calypso, where clever, witty lyrics matter more than anything else.

Tamboo-bamboo bands

After emancipation, the slaves were allowed to join in with the official Carnival celebrations, and they turned a rather sedate Christian holiday into a rowdy festival. This gradually grew in size – and became more and more violent – until the British police felt they had to step in and try to suppress the fighting. The Africans' retaliation led to two days of rioting in Port of Spain (the capital of Trinidad) in 1881 (now known as the **Canboulay riots**). As a result, stick fighting and the use of African-style drums were banned by the officials.

To circumvent this ban, the revellers invented **tamboo-bamboo bands**. These used different lengths and widths of bamboo to produce a variety of sounds. The resulting band was unmelodic, but offered a variety of untuned pitch and timbre with which to fashion rhythmic music. YouTube video 'Calypso 1: tamboo bamboo' shows a modern-day re-enactment of a tamboo-bamboo band in Trinidad.

Calypso

Meanwhile, towards the end of the 19th century, the songs of the black people in Trinidad evolved from being in French patois to **Creole English**. The words retained their focus on political gossip and scandal, social criticism and satire, and topical events. The songs were often accompanied by an instrument imported from nearby Venezuela: the **cuatro**, a small guitar. Songs would often be built around a short, repeating phrase that the chorus sang in response to more narrative lines from the main solo singer.

These features can be heard in the calypso *Edward the VIII* by Rufus Caresser (alias 'Lord Caresser'), a fascinating period piece from 1937 that reflects on the abdication of a British king from a Caribbean island that was, at the time, still part of his empire. You can listen to this through Spotify or the YouTube video 'Calypso 2: Caresser'.

Listen out for the repeating refrain of the backing singers, with its highly idiomatic use of syncopations:

58

Edward VIII came to the throne on the death of his father, George V, on 20 January 1936. As the year passed, it became apparent that the new king intended to marry Wallis Simpson, a twice-divorced American lady. At the time it was considered unacceptable that the king, as head of the Church of England, could be married to a divorcee. On 10 December 1926, Edward abdicated his throne and became the Duke of Windsor, living in exile in France. His younger brother became King George VI. Edward duly married Wallis Simpson; their marriage lasted 35 years until the Duke died in 1972.

In the 1930s, the fledgling **recording industry** played an important role in spreading calypso's popularity, both nationally and internationally. Many calypsonians started to record albums in America. American jazz also influenced the calypso sound, and brass instruments became a prominent feature of most bands.

Calypsonians are known by their nicknames, which are usually chosen to give the singer an intimidating, larger-than-life stature. Some of the most significant calypsonians since the 1930s have been:

* **Attila the Hun:** born Raymond Quevedo in Trinidad in 1892. He was one of the first to take calypso to the USA when he toured there in 1934. A prominent singer in the 1930s and 40s, he then went into politics. He died in 1962. One of his most popular songs is *FDR in Trinidad*, written in 1936 to commemorate President Roosevelt's visit to Trinidad (YouTube video 'Calypso 3: Attila').
* **Lord Invader:** born Rupert Westmore Grant in Trinidad in 1914. He grew up in the countryside, moving to Port of Spain in 1937. Along with Attila the Hun, he was important in promoting calypso in the USA, spending a few years living in New York. He died in 1961. His most famous song is *Rum and Coca-Cola*, written about the local women who were prostituting themselves for the American soldiers (YouTube video 'Calypso 4: Invader').
* **Lord Kitchener:** born Aldwyn Roberts in Trinidad in 1922. He emigrated to England in 1948, returning to Trinidad in 1962. One of his favourite topics was cricket, leading to songs such as *Cricket Champions* in 1967 (YouTube video 'Calypso 5: Kitchener'). He died in 2000 and there is a statue of him in Port of Spain.
* **Lord Melody:** born Fitzroy Alexander in Trinidad in 1926 and raised in an orphanage. Among his songs were *Berlin on a Donkey*, which lampooned Adolf Hitler, and the self-deprecating *Boo Boo Man* (YouTube video 'Calypso 6: Melody'). He died in 1988.

✱ **Calypso Rose**: born McCartha Linda Sandy-Lewis in Tobago in 1940. She was one of the first famous female calypsonians, and wrote over 800 songs including *Fire Fire* (YouTube video 'Calypso 7: Rose').

✱ **The Mighty Sparrow**: born Slinger Francisco in Grenada in 1935, his family moved to Trinidad at the age of 1. Along with Lord Kitchener he is one of the most successful calypsonians, winning many competitions and accolades. Sparrow's lyrics are often quite earthy or ironic, and he has also tackled political issues with numbers such as *Congo Man* – a satirical, witty look at African roots (YouTube video 'Calypso 8: Sparrow').

The rise of the steel band

By the 1930s, the tamboo-bamboo bands were now using a dazzling array of objects to create additional percussive timbres, including soap boxes, biscuit tins, dustbins, gin bottles and various bits of iron such as car brake discs. By the end of the decade, metal containers had largely replaced the use of bamboo sticks. Various musicians – such as Winston 'Spree' Simon of the John John tamboo-bamboo band – then started to experiment with denting the containers to produce different notes.

The US navy arrived in Trinidad in 1941, and part of the Americans' impact on the island was the introduction of large **oil drums** (typically with a 55 gallon capacity). These quickly became the primary material out of which to make steel pans, and during the 1940s considerable developments were made in the creation and tuning of these instruments.

The new sound soon caught on. In 1951, the Trinidad All-Steel Percussion Orchestra was formed to represent Trinidad at the Festival of Britain in London, and by the 1970s there were more than 200 steel bands on the island, involving over 5,000 people.

The steel band has since spread around the Caribbean, and it is now the iconic sound of the region, sponsored by governments and promoted by the tourist industry. Antigua, for example, has a particularly vibrant steel-band scene. To watch a typically exuberant steel-band performance from Trinidad, see YouTube video 'Calypso 9: steel band'.

Calypso competitions

There is a strong competitive edge to the Carnival celebrations in Trinidad today, which harks all the way back to the slaves' stick fighting in their Canboulay festival. Calypso is primarily performed as part of the various competitions that have sprung up to promote and celebrate the genre. The main one of these is the **Calypso Monarch** competition, for which the winner in 2012 received $1 million. The basic structure of this competition is as follows:

* The competition effectively begins before Christmas, when the **tents** hold auditions to find singers to perform on their bills in the run up to Carnival. (The tents were originally simple bamboo structures that provided shelter from the rains, but now refer to larger performance spaces such as theatres and community halls.)
* During the course of the calypso season, a judging panel will visit every tent and select 24 singers to take part in the semi-final.
* This is held in front of 30,000 people at Skinner Park, a sporting venue in San Fernando. Each singer is allowed to perform two songs, which are judged on the following categories: lyrics, melody, originality, rendition and presentation.
* 11 singers go through to the final (which always includes the defending champion); the winner is crowned as the Calypso Monarch. You can watch the 2012 winner, Duane O'Connor, in YouTube video 'Calypso 10: O'Connor'.

For the steel bands, the main competition is the **Panorama**. This follows a similar format to the Calypso Monarch competition, with preliminary rounds, semi-finals and finals. The 12 finalists are whittled down from around 80 different bands. Each band is allowed to perform one calypso of their choice that can last for up to 10 minutes, and is judged on the following categories: arrangement, general performance, tone and rhythm. YouTube video 'Calypso 11: Panorama' is of the 2012 winners, the Trinidad All Stars.

Both the Calypso Monarch and Panorama competitions have sprouted 'Junior' versions for children. Calypsonians can begin honing their craft at a very young age: YouTube video 'Calypso 12: Duncan' is a performance of *Doh Waste It* by Aaron Duncan, who won the Junior Calypso Monarch in 2010 at the age of 6, with a song about following his mother's advice to not waste resources such as electricity and water.

CHARACTERISTIC FEATURES OF THE STYLE

Common features of calypso include:

* A duple metre
* An upbeat tempo and major key (although the older calypsos were often slower and minor)
* Simple, diatonic progressions mainly consisting of chords I, IV and V
* A verse-and-chorus structure that is usually strophic
* Melodic lines played in parallel 3rds
* Offbeat accompaniment patterns, such as:

* Syncopated melodic lines, such as:

The lyrics of calypso are characterised by themes such as:

* Political comment
* Satirical treatment of scandal
* Popular local topics (such as cricket)
* Romantic tales, often involving double entendres.

LISTENING EXAMPLE

Jean and Dinah is a well-known calypso that was initially a hit in 1956 for The Mighty Sparrow. The song is representative of the type of social commentary that is at the heart of the calypso tradition. The lyrics reflect on the closure of the American bases on the island, and the hope that Trinidadian men would no longer lose their girls to the 'Yankees' (not least due to the high levels of prostitution the bases encouraged).

There are various versions of this song available; the following timeline is for the recording by Lord Superior on the album *Calypso at Dirty Jim's*, available on Spotify. You can listen to the original version by The Mighty Sparrow in YouTube video 'Calypso 13: Jean and Dinah'.

Introduction	
0:00	Trumpets and saxes in parallel 3rds playing a syncopated melody. Accompanied by piano, guitar, bass guitar and congas.
Verse 1	
0:10	Lord Superior sings the first verse, which describes the effects of the 'Yankees' leaving town. Accompanied by walking bass, piano vamp, guitar strumming and brass interjections/countermelodies.
Refrain 1	
0:29	Lord Superior is joined by a female backing chorus to sing the refrain, which includes the first mention of Jean and Dinah (who give the song its name).
Interlude 1	
0:48	Instrumental version of the refrain: trumpets and saxes in parallel 3rds.
Verse 2	
1:07	The second verse mentions how the night clubs have emptied as a result of the Americans leaving.
Refrain 2	
1:26	Vocal refrain with backing chorus.
Interlude 2	
1:45	Instrumental version of the refrain.
Verse 3	
2:03	The third verse describes how the women always preferred the Yankees to the local men.
Refrain 3	
2:22	Vocal refrain with backing chorus.
Interlude 3	
2:41	Improvised trumpet solo with some chromaticism (displaying the influence of American jazz).
Verse 4	
2:59	The fourth verse describes how the local men are going to rule again now the Americans have gone.

Refrain 4	
3:17	Vocal refrain with backing chorus.
Coda	
3:35	Instrumental version of the refrain, cut short before the last line.

You might like to give your students the following questions to focus their listening:

1. What instruments are heard in the introduction? (Saxes, trumpets, guitar, bass guitar, piano, congas)
2. In the first refrain, the brass play a short five-note riff after the singer's second and fourth lines. Which instrument takes over this riff in the first interlude? (The piano)
3. In which interlude does Lord Superior say 'alright'? (Interlude 1)
4. In which verse does Lord Superior mention the empty night clubs? (Verse 2)
5. In which refrain does Lord Superior not sing 'Jean and Dinah', leaving this line to the backing singers? (Refrain 2)
6. In which interlude does Lord Superior sing a long sustained note? (Interlude 2)
7. Which interlude features a big trumpet improvisation? (Interlude 3)
8. How does the coda differ to the interludes? (There is no final phrase)

You can listen to a version of this song played on steel pans on the album *Toucans Play Calypso*, which is also available on Spotify. The structure for this arrangement is:

Refrain	Refrain	Verse	Refrain	Verse	Refrain	Improv.	Improv.	Verse	Refrain	Refrain	Coda
0:00	0:21	0:42	1:02	1:23	1:43	2:04	2:23	2:43	3:02	3:23	3:44

The harmonisation of the refrain in this version might be worth some focus. The first 8 bars use a classic I–V–V–I progression; then there is a falling chromatic bass line in bars 10–12. Bar 13 is in unison before a I–V–I cadence rounds off the refrain:

1	2	3	4	5	6	7	8	9	10	11	12	13	14	15	16
C	C	G	G	G	G	C	C	C	C/B♭	F/A	F/A♭	C	C	G	C

The bass line in the refrain is also highly characteristic of calypso, both in terms of its triadic nature and the syncopated ♪ ♪ ♪ rhythm.

You may wish to ask your students to work out the chord sequence for the verse as, in true calypso fashion, it only uses chords I, IV and V. In addition, the bass pans play the root of each chord on the first beat of the bar. The progression is:

1	2	3	4	5	6	7	8	9	10	11	12	13	14	15	16
C	C	F	C	C	C	G	G	C	C	F	C	C	C	G	C

This progression also underpins the improvised sections (which make use of the flattened third and seventh).

PERFORMING

Water Come a Me Eye is a traditional calypso from another Caribbean island: Jamaica. Rather than having a social or political theme, this is a tender love song that is structured with a call-and-response design. The arrangement provided on the book website could be performed by just piano and voices (maybe with percussion); alternatively the extra staves provide scope for adapting this piece for a variety of instruments – even steel pans!

COMPOSING

Calypso offers a good opportunity for young composers. The style has a simple harmonic palette (primary triads alone are very suitable), a straightforward metre ($\frac{2}{4}$ is ideal), and short, often conjunct or arpeggio-based melodic phrases. The focus should be on creating a melody that uses syncopated rhythms and fits with the three primary triads.

Step one: choosing a topic

Students should choose a topic for their calypso first. Calypsos are frequently based on current events and news; bearing this in mind, suitable topics might be:

* A recent event at school or in the local area
* A story in the news
* Part of a daily routine
* A day out during the holidays.

Step two: writing the lyrics

A good first step for your students is to think of a short refrain that can act as the recurring line which everyone joins in with throughout the song. There also need to be four other phrases, each of similar length, that alternate with the refrain. For example:

Refrain line: All my friends are coming too.

Lyrics: At half term I'm going to London,
All my friends are coming too.
We are going to a musical,
All my friends are coming too.
It's my birthday outing,
All my friends are coming too.
I am so excited,
All my friends are coming too.

Step three: composing the melody

To begin with, your students should choose a major key (probably one with a simple key signature) and work out the three primary chords: tonic, subdominant and dominant. It might also be helpful to work out the dominant 7th.

The next step is to create a melody for the first line. This should:

* Only use notes from the tonic chord
* Last for two bars.

Your students can then write a (largely) stepwise melody for the refrain. This should:

* Fit a chord progression of V^7–I
* End on a note that is in the tonic chord
* Include a syncopated rhythm.

For the second line, they can either adapt the tune of the first line to fit the different words, or write a different tune but still follow the same rules as used for line 1. Similarly, the refrain can either be identical to how it appears at the end of line 1, or it can be a different melody (with the same rhythm) that still fits the V⁷–I progression.

Moving on to the third line, the melody here needs to fit a IV–I pattern, with one bar for each chord. The refrain will remain the same (your students might now have two different melodies for it, in which case they can use the first one this time). The fourth line should be very similar to the third, varied as necessary to fit the different words. The refrain then appears one last time to finish off the song.

Since this makes for a short piece of music, it might be a very good project to use as the basis for a lesson on getting to grips with notation software such as Sibelius. There will only be 16 bars of music to input, but certain issues are likely to arise for each student:

* How to input ties (due to the syncopations)
* How to input lyrics
* How to input chord symbols.

Your students might aim for something along these lines:

Step four: adding an accompaniment

This project could be undertaken so that students only have to focus on rhythm and melody; you could fill out the harmony yourself during a performance by playing the chord progression on keyboard or guitar. Alternatively, some of your students may like to compose their own accompaniment. They could add a bass line that falls on the root of the chord at the start of each bar. The chords could be strummed by a guitar, ideally emphasising the offbeats. The addition of percussion such as shakers could help to create an idiomatic sense of colour.

CROSS-CURRICULAR LINKS

Citizenship link: the transatlantic slave trade was integral to the development of calypso music, and your students could explore this further by investigating the history and effects of the slave trade, and William Wilberforce's role in its abolition. Students could also learn about the various ways in which slavery still manifests itself today (such as through bonded labour and trafficking): the website www.antislavery.org is a good place to start.

History/politics link: since the start of the 20th century, calypsonians have written songs in response to topical issues and contemporary events. Investigating the backgrounds to some of these calypsos – such as *P.A.Y.E* and *Barak the Magnificent* by The Mighty Sparrow – can be a very interesting way of learning more about the events that Trinidadians have deemed to be newsworthy over the years.

RESOURCES

Workshops

Steel-pan workshops are currently very popular in UK schools, and as a result there are many organisations across the UK who could run a steel-pan workshop for your students. Your local music education hub may be able to organise this, or alternatively you could search for providers online. CultureMix, based in Berkshire, are worth mentioning here for the range of services that they provide, and the extra background material on steel-pan music that can be accessed from their website.

Books, CDs and DVDs

* *Carnival Music in Trinidad* by Shannon Dudley (Oxford University Press, 2003): a short book that provides a good overview of calypso and steel-pan music, accompanied by a CD.
* *Carnival, Canboulay and Calypso* by John Cowley (Cambridge University Press, 1996): a book that details the history of calypso music from

its origins in the Canboulay festivals to the first decades of the 20th century.

* *Teach & Play Steel Pans* by Mike Simpson (Rhinegold Education, 2012): a book of five steel-pan pieces designed for school use, accompanied by a DVD.

* *Legends of Calypso* (Arc Music), *The Rough Guide to Calypso Gold* and *The Rough Guide to Calypso and Soca* (World Music Network): three compilation CDs that provide a good introduction to calypso music.

* *Calypso @ Dirty Jim's* (Dynamo Production): a documentary about the 'golden age' of calypso, featuring performances from calypsonians such as The Mighty Sparrow and Calypso Rose, who frequented the famous nightclub Dirty Jim's Swizzle Club in Port of Spain.

CELTIC MUSIC

WHY TEACH CELTIC MUSIC?

The term 'Celtic music' refers to the musical traditions of the Celts and their descendents, who today live in eight main regions across Europe: Ireland, Scotland, Wales, the Isle of Man, Cornwall, Brittany (France) and Galicia and Asturias (Spain). Each region has its own local cultural traits and distinctive features, and it is beyond the scope of this book to tackle all eight styles of Celtic music. Instead, this chapter will focus on traditional Irish music, as it is arguably the best known of all Celtic styles, and the one with which you and your students are most likely to have some familiarity.

Some will consider Celtic music too close to home to count as 'world music', but it is this familiarity that can make it a great starting place from which to explore more unfamiliar and far-flung styles of music. Celtic music also has a lively, infectious nature that can lead to fun performance projects, and a fairly basic structure (in its most traditional format) that can lead to straightforward composition projects.

A BRIEF HISTORY

The Celts

In its modern use, the term 'Celtic' refers to cultures whose language can be traced back to the ancient Celtic peoples of Western Europe, who thrived during the **late European Iron Age** (around 600 BC). The Celts inhabited an extensive part of Europe during this time, before they were pushed into northern Europe by the Roman Empire around the start of the first millennium.

The Celtic languages divide into two families with common features: **Goidelic** refers to Irish, Scots Gaelic and Manx (Isle of Man), and **Brythonic** refers to Welsh, Cornish and Breton (Brittany). In 2010, there were about 1.4 million speakers of Celtic languages spread around world.

Due to the emigration of Irish, Scots and Cornish during the 19th–20th centuries, Celtic cultural heritage and practice is evident in certain parts of North America, Canada, Australia and New Zealand. In fact, modern Celtic regional and national identity is strong and there is often a sense of camaraderie between the different Celtic regions. Celtic culture, including music, also continues to thrive and develop in these areas.

Gaelic Ireland

Music played an important **ceremonial role** in the lives of the ancient Celts. There was a strong tradition of epic song, which told of heroic feats and battles. Celtic warriors went into battle singing, accompanied by the rattling of their weapons. One of the best-documented musical instruments was the **carnyx:** a very long bronze trumpet with the bell shaped like an animal's head, which was played vertically (the bell being lifted upward). It was widespread in Britain and France, and dates from about 300 BC. It is thought that the carnyx was used in battle to frighten the enemy. YouTube video 'Celtic 1: carnyx' shows a demonstration on a modern reproduction of the instrument.

Up until about 1600, Ireland was ruled by the **Gaels**: speakers of the Goidelic languages. Under their reign, Ireland was broken up into numerous clans with regional kings, along with a system of nobles who ruled the country. Little is known about folk music from this time, but it is thought that music was a major feature of the **aristocratic courts**, with the cruit (harp) being the main instrument used. The piopai and ciusli (bagpipes) and the fidli (an early bowed string instrument) were also common.

Before the introduction of Christianity in the 5th century, the Gaels were a pagan society and their druids were held in very high esteem. The 6th century saw the gradual adoption of **Christianity** and with it, Christian music. The 12th century saw the arrival of the Anglo-Normans from Wales, who posed the greatest threat to the Gaels. However, they managed to coexist until 1600, and this marked a strong period of feudal patronage for the Irish poet-musicians or bards.

Due to Ireland's commercial potential and the risk of the country being used as an invading post by Spain, the Crown of Ireland Act brought the country under the rule of **King Henry VIII** in **1542**. The Gaelic feudal system ended with the fleeing of the Irish Aristocracy (known as 'The Flight of the Earls') in 1607.

Patronage and dancing masters

With the colonisation of the country by English-speaking settlers, the Gaelic aristocracy declined and the new Anglo-Irish wealthy classes became patrons of the arts instead: musicians would travel between their houses to perform at social functions, weddings and funerals.

The most celebrated of these musicians was the composer and harpist **Turlough O'Carolan** (1670–1738). He was blinded by smallpox at an early age, but with a guide he travelled the country for most of his life, performing and composing music. He is considered by many to be Ireland's greatest national composer. Very few of his song lyrics survived, but many of his melodies did: you can hear some of his music in YouTube video 'Celtic 2: O'Carolan'. He bridged the gap between traditional and art music, drawing influence from Italian composers of the day such as Geminiani.

In the 1780s, travelling **dancing masters** started to become fashionable. They would arrive in a new area, hire a barn and set up a temporary school. For a fee they taught dances to both groups and individuals. The dancing was generally accompanied by a fiddle and the uilleann pipes (a type of Irish bagpipe). This dancing craze played a large part in establishing the jigs, reels, polkas and hornpipes that are the mainstay of traditional Irish music today.

The Great Famine and British rule

In 1800, the **Acts of Union** created the United Kingdom of Great Britain and Ireland. During the second half of the 1840s, Ireland suffered through the **Great Famine**. The decimation of the potato crop during this time – which was the staple food of the poorer classes – led to the deaths of about one million Irish, with a further million emigrating (many to North America). This had a devastating effect on many aspects of Irish life, including the arts. One interesting element of its legacy is that it provided the inspiration for numerous songs about emigration, which is a theme that has remained common throughout the Celtic diaspora.

After a series of negotiations with a British government that was increasingly disinterested in union, the **Irish Free State** was established in 1922 and self-rule began. The six counties of the north remained part of the UK, while the 26 of the south became independent. This was immediately followed by a year-long **civil war** between those content with the British monarch remaining head of state and those opposed to it. This eventually led to the Republic of Ireland Act in 1948, which removed the British monarch from Irish affairs altogether.

The folk revival

The 1960s saw a strong resurgence in the interest in folk music throughout the UK, following a similar movement in America. The founding of numerous folk clubs and strong record sales allowed folk musicians to turn professional, touring extensively and enjoying the financial rewards of popularity. In Ireland, groups such as The Chieftains, The Bothy Band and Planxty brought traditional Celtic music into the concert hall, introducing it to a wider (and often younger) audience. Extravagant stage shows based on Celtic culture, such as *Riverdance*, have extended the music's reach from the club and pub session to the arts mainstream.

Irish traditional music has also been appropriated by popular musicians. **Celtic rock**, for example, has become hugely popular since the 1970s; this refers to bands with a standard rock line-up that incorporate traditional Celtic tunes into their music. Thin Lizzy were one of the first bands to branch into Celtic rock: their hit *Whisky in the Jar*, for example, was a cover of a well-known traditional Irish song (see YouTube video 'Celtic 3: Thin Lizzy'). Other bands that have since followed in their footsteps with great success include The Horslips, Clannad, Moving Hearts and The Corrs.

INSTRUMENTATION

A wide range of instruments are used in Irish Celtic music. Some have been present in folk music for hundreds of years, while others have only been accepted into the tradition more recently. This section introduces some of the most common.

Uilleann pipes: rather than being mouth blown like the Scottish bagpipes, these are powered by a set of small bellows held under one arm. There are a number of pipes that each have a different role in the music: the 'chanter' is used to play the melody, the 'drones' provide a sustained droning accompaniment, and the 'regulators' can be used to create simple chords. The combination of pumping the bellows, playing the melody with both hands and adding chords in with the wrists makes the uilleann pipes a very challenging instrument to master. YouTube video 'Celtic 4: uilleann pipes' is a performance by the master piper Cillian Vallely.

Celtic harp: perhaps the instrument most associated with Celtic music, the harp is one of the official national emblems of Ireland. The Celtic harp is smaller than the concert harp, and comes without pedals. Instead, strings can be raised or lowered a semitone by a series of levers that are attached to the top of the harp. You can watch Irish harpist Laoise Kelly perform in YouTube video 'Celtic 5: harp'.

Fiddle: this is the folk name for the violin. It is essentially the same instrument, although some players favour a looser bow tension and more relaxed posture. It is one of the most commonly played instruments in Celtic music. The Irish fiddler Martin Hayes performs in YouTube video 'Celtic 6: fiddle'.

Irish flute: this instrument retains the early 'simple-system' design of European flutes from the Classical period. Many Irish flutes are wooden and keyless (so the notes are just produced by covering the holes with your fingers), although some flutes do incorporate metal keys. This instrument has a softer, breathier tone than the orchestral flute: listen for example to the Irish flautist Matt Molloy in YouTube video 'Celtic 7: flute'.

Button accordion: often just referred to as the 'box', this is a type of accordion where the melody is played on buttons rather than a piano-style keyboard. Each button produces two different notes (or chords): one when the bellows are pulled out and another when they're pushed in. This push-pull nature of the instrument tends to give it a strong rhythmic drive. You can watch the Irish player Seamus Begley in YouTube video 'Celtic 8: accordion.'

Tin whistle: this instrument just consists of a simple metal tube with six finger holes and a recorder-like mouthpiece. A range of sizes in different keys are available, the most common being tuned to D. It is often the first instrument that a student of Irish music learns to play tunes on before taking up another. The Irish player Mary Bergin performs in YouTube video 'Celtic 9: whistle'.

Bouzouki: a Greek lute that was introduced to the Irish music scene in the 1960s by the mandolin player Johnny Moynihan. As a result of its adoption by Irish musicians, the design of the instrument changed: the Irish version now has a flat-backed body and a shorter neck than its Greek counterpart. YouTube video 'Celtic 10: bouzouki' is a performance by the Irish player Donal Lunny.

Acoustic guitar: this became popular as an accompanying instrument in the 1960s, and today is the most common 'backing' instrument in Irish folk music.

The 'electro-acoustic' version is generally favoured for amplification. In YouTube video 'Celtic 11: guitar', Paul Brady demonstrates the guitar's use in traditional Irish music.

Bodhrán: a circular, wooden frame drum with a skin on one side (typically goat). It can be played with the hand or more commonly with a *cipín* (a short wooden stick). The drum was traditionally associated with St. Stephen's Day (Boxing Day) celebrations in Ireland, where its use was quite basic. However, since the 1960s it has developed into a dynamic and technically skilful percussion instrument. Colm Murphy gives a bodhrán solo in YouTube video 'Celtic 12: bodhrán'.

CHARACTERISTIC FEATURES OF THE STYLE

Instrumental music

Celtic music is essentially an **oral tradition:** it is primarily passed down by ear with the student learning through imitation. Collections such as *The Dance Music of Ireland: O'Neill's 1001* provide musicians with basic notation, but they don't include ornamentation, articulation or other nuances of the music. They are considered to provide simple skeletal representations as an aid to learning and a way of preserving and transmitting music.

Exact styles of playing vary between regions, and it is the personal transmission from teacher to student that allows a certain style in any one area to be established and maintained. The County Donegal style of fiddle playing, for example, is known for its sparse ornamentation, ringing open strings and fast pace. In contrast, fiddlers in County Clare play more slowly and with much more ornamentation. This means that musicians from different regions may play the same tune in very different ways.

The majority of Irish instrumental music consists of tunes that were originally used to accompany **dancing** (such as Irish stepdance, which has become internationally famous thanks to the popularity of the *Riverdance* show – see YouTube video 'Celtic 13: Riverdance'). This means that most tunes are performed at a lively tempo with a strong sense of rhythm, and the metre of the music is dictated by what type of dance it traditionally accompanies. The following list describes the main features of this type of music:

* The most common dance tunes are jigs ($\frac{6}{8}$), reels ($\frac{4}{4}$), hornpipes ($\frac{4}{4}$), polkas ($\frac{2}{4}$) and waltzes ($\frac{3}{4}$).
* Most tunes consist of a near-constant quaver movement.
* Tunes are frequently built up in 8-bar sections. Each section is repeated before moving on to the next one; at the end, the whole tune is repeated from the beginning. A typical structure, therefore, would be AABBCC (repeat).
* Tunes are typically in major or minor keys, but many show a modal influence with a flattened seventh (the Dorian and Mixolydian modes are common, for example).
* Players will add ornamentation to a tune, particularly on the repeats. This may include 'trebles' (triplets), 'cuts' (grace notes) and 'rolls' (turns). The amount of ornamentation varies between regional styles.
* Harmonic accompaniment – which is often provided by the guitar, piano or bouzouki – is traditionally quite simple, with much use of the primary chords (I, IV and V).

A typical Irish tune that exhibits most of these characteristics is the jig *Banish Misfortune*, notated below. This tune is usually described as being in the Mixolydian mode, although note the extra C♯s that also suggest D major. The tune has an AABBCC structure (with each section consisting of 8 bars).

YouTube videos 'Celtic 14: Banish 1' and 'Celtic 15: Banish 2' give two performances of this jig that highlight some of the different approaches that musicians might take to adding in ornamentation and varying the tune.

Further examples

The musicians and YouTube videos mentioned below will provide you with a good starting point for exploring Celtic instrumental music further.

* ✽ **The Chieftains** are a traditional Irish band who have won six Grammy awards and helped to popularise Irish music around the world. Formed in Dublin in 1962, they were one of the first groups to arrange traditional music formally, laying the foundations for many bands that followed. See YouTube video 'Celtic 16: Chieftains'.
* ✽ **The Bothy Band** were only together for four years in the second half of the 1970s, but they were hugely influential and helped to introduce Irish music to a wider, younger audience. One of their defining characteristics was the use of the clavinet (electric harpsichord), which gave their music a modern sound. See YouTube video 'Celtic 17: Bothy Band'.
* ✽ **Liam O'Flynn**, a uilleann piper, is recognised as being one of the most successful Irish traditional musicians on the international stage. See YouTube video 'Celtic 18: O'Flynn'.
* ✽ **John Doherty** was a renowned fiddler from Donegal who died in 1980. He travelled extensively around Ireland to perform his music and was sought out by a number of folk collectors, including the famous American folklorist Alan Lomax. See YouTube video 'Celtic 19: Doherty'.

Folk sessions

In addition to being used to accompany dancing, instrumental tunes are most commonly performed at informal gatherings called 'sessions', which usually take place in a pub. The session is one of the main performance opportunities for the traditional musician, and it is here that tunes are swapped and ensemble skills honed. Generally, players take it in turns to decide which tunes to play and the majority are known by all. Tunes tend to be performed in sets, with two or three being played together in a row. YouTube video 'Celtic 20: session' will give you a feel for the typical Irish session.

Vocal music

Ireland has a rich song tradition that stretches back over centuries. One of the oldest styles of singing is **sean-nós** (or 'old style' in Irish). This unaccompanied, highly ornamented style of singing – with lyrics sung in Irish Gaelic – has enjoyed something of a resurgence in popularity in recent years. Listen for example to the singer Bríd Ní Mhaoilchiaráin in YouTube video 'Celtic 21: sean-nós'.

After the Flight of the Earls in 1607, Gaelic culture and language were discouraged under British rule, and Irish Gaelic has since become a second language to most Irish people. The singing of songs in Irish Gaelic has primarily been maintained in the few areas where it is still spoken as a first language (such as Connemara in West Ireland, which is where Bríd Ní Mhaoilchiaráin comes from).

English has traditionally been the language of Celtic ballads and most contemporary Irish song. In the 18th to 19th centuries, **broadside ballads** were very popular in Ireland. These narrative songs were printed on inexpensive paper and sold on street corners, with the vendor singing the tune to attract customers. Ballad singing is still a major part of Irish vocal music. One well-known example is *The Fields of Athenry* (see YouTube video 'Celtic 22: Athenry'). This ballad was written in the 1970s and tells the story of a young man who stole food for his starving family during the Great Famine.

Ireland has its own tradition of scat-like singing called **lilting** (also known as **mouth music**), where instrumental dance tunes are sung to meaningless vocables. This form of music is traditionally used to accompany dance. See for example YouTube video 'Celtic 23: lilting'.

LISTENING EXAMPLE

The Cat She Went a Hunting is a humorous Irish song written by the singer-songwriter Sonny Condell in the 1970s. The timeline below accompanies a cover version of this song by the Irish band Dervish, who were formed in 1989 and have since become internationally successful. The song can be found on their 2008 album *Travelling Show* (available on iTunes and Spotify); you can watch a live performance of the song in YouTube video 'Celtic 24: Dervish'.

Introduction	
0:00	Bodhrán plays a jig rhythm incorporating triplets.
0:03	Bouzouki enters with an ostinato bass line.
0:11	Button accordion joins in playing minor chords in a jig rhythm. Mandola adds a harmony line to the bouzouki ostinato.

0:19	Flute repeats a simple 4-bar phrase while the violin plays a tonic drone.
0:26	Flute and violin play the jig melody.
Verse 1	
0:45	Move to the tonic major key. Voice enters accompanied by chords and countermelodies played on bouzouki and mandola. *The cat she went a-hunting and found the barn a-blazing* *And back she's come a-calling, a-calling, a-calling* *Wake up farm boys! The barn is burning down!* *And the rats came out in their hundreds, the cat she caught a-plenty* *She's got the artful dodger, the dodger, the dodger* *She spied him in the burning hay, the barn is burning down!*
Chorus	
1:12	Bouzouki doubles the vocal melody in a lower octave, and mandola plays a countermelody. *Now the cat she had to hide her face behind the rat she's eating* *So as not to show a smirk and later get a beating* Bouzouki and mandola switch to chords. *The farmer trips on his dungarees and he falls down the stairs* Bodhrán plays a 'falling' rumbling sound.
Instrumental interlude	
1:24	Fiddle, flute and bouzouki play the original jig tune (in the tonic minor) twice; the second time through, the fiddle plays a variation of the tune a minor 3rd higher.
Verse 2	
1:41	Return to the tonic major key. *The fire brigade is coming with farm children singing* *And we'll be sipping on boiled eggs, on boiled eggs, on boiled eggs* Flute adds a countermelody. *So open the cage and hose us down we'll make it a dozen a day* *But the roof is starting to crumble, sparks go up in the night sky* *The dogs are wearing their tails down, their tails down, their tails down* *The boys are making a chain in the yard and they're passing the pails along*

Chorus	
2:07	Bouzouki doubles the vocal melody in a lower octave and mandola plays a countermelody. *Now the cat she had to hide her face behind the rat she's eating* *So as not to show a smirk and later get a beating* Bouzouki and mandola play chords. *The farmer trips on his dungarees and he falls down the stairs* Descending melodic 'falling' motif accompanied by bodhrán.
Instrumental interlude	
2:21	Flute and fiddle play interweaving melody lines, accompanied by mandola, bouzouki and accordion chords.
2:44	Interlude continues with the verse melody played by the flute, with the fiddle harmonising.
2:53	Extra percussion added (djembe, toms and cymbal). Flute and violin play the chorus melody between the vocal lines. *Wake up farm boys! The barn is burning down!* *Wake up farm boys! The barn is burning down!*
3:09	Flute and fiddle play the chorus melody.
End section	
3:22	Bouzouki and mandola play chords and countermelodies; bodhrán and jaw harp accompany. *The cat she went a-hunting and found the barn a-blazing* *And back she's come a-calling, a-calling, a-calling* Flute and violin add a countermelody. *And back she's come a-calling, a-calling, a-calling* *And back she's come a-calling, a-calling, a-calling*
3:39	Begins to slow down for the finish; final tremolo chord at 3:46.

After listening to *The Cat She Went a Hunting*, you could test your students' understanding of the song with these questions:

1. The fiddle is the folk-music term for which instrument? (The violin)
2. Name three of the other instruments heard in this song that are commonly found in traditional Irish music. (Any three of: bodhrán, bouzouki, button accordion, flute, jaw harp, mandola)
3. What time signature is this song in? (⁶/₈)
4. What is a drone? Pinpoint one place in the song where you can hear one. (A sustained note that is held in one part while a melody is heard above it. The fiddle plays a drone at 0:19)
5. This song is sung in English. Name another language that is also heard in Irish Celtic music. (Irish Gaelic)
6. What happens to the tonality of the music when the voice first enters? (It changes from minor to major)
7. At 2:14 'the farmer trips on his dungarees and he falls down the stairs': how is this illustrated in the music? (There is a descending melodic figure accompanied by the bodhrán)
8. At 3:09 do the fiddle and flute play the melody to the verse or the chorus? (The chorus)
9. Why do you think the cat was smirking? (Because the fire had cleared all of the rats out of the barn, giving the cat an easy meal)

PERFORMING

Use any melody instruments available to perform the reel below called *Far From Home*. Your students may wish to add ornamentation and small variations to the melody once they are confident with it.

As Dervish did in *The Cat She Went a Hunting*, you could combine this instrumental tune with an Irish song. The well-known song *I'll Tell Me Ma* nicely complements the reel above (see YouTube video 'Celtic 25: Tell Me Ma') – verses of the song, notated below, could be alternated with playings of the reel.

2. *Albert Mooney says he loves her, all the boys are fightin' for her.*
   Knock at the door and ring at the bell, saying oh my true love, are you well.
   Out she comes as white as snow, rings on her fingers, bells on her toes.
   Old Jenny Murphy says she'll die, if she doesn't get the fella with the roving eye.

3. *Let the wind and the rain and the hail blow high, and the snow come travellin' through the sky.*
   She's as sweet as apple pie, she'll get her own lad by and by.
   When she gets a lad of her own, she won't tell her ma when she gets home.
   Let them all come as they will, for it's Albert Mooney she loves still.

You could use the chord symbols given above to create a basic accompaniment for the song, including a simple bass line. Your class could split into singers and instrumentalists so all can easily be involved; the singers could improvise basic percussion parts during the reel.

COMPOSING

Dance tune

The following tune called *The Kesh Jig* (YouTube video 'Celtic 26: Kesh Jig')
is a typical Celtic tune that your students could use as a template to compose
their own.

Using this tune as an example, your students could follow the rules below to
compose their own traditional jig.

1. The time signature should be ⁶⁄₈ and the key signature G major.
2. The jig should be in two sections, each 8 bars long.
3. The melody should be either (a) in the Dorian mode, (b) in the Mixolydian
   mode, or (c) based on a hexatonic scale (like *The Kesh Jig*, which omits
   the note C).
4. Quaver movement should dominate, with a few crotchets and dotted
   crotchets added for variation.
5. To provide a bit of contrast between the two sections, the first could
   consist of lower notes with a little less quaver movement, and the second
   could consist of higher notes with a little more quaver movement.
6. Each section should end with a crotchet or dotted crotchet on the tonic
   note of the scale.
7. Using chords I, IV and V, an accompaniment could be added to the jig.
   Each section should end with a tonic chord.

Irish song

We mentioned at the start of this chapter that emigration is a theme that commonly occurs in Irish song. Listen for example to *Paddy Green's Shamrock Shore* (YouTube video 'Celtic 27: Green'). As a class, you could research and discuss the experience of the Irish people who emigrated to America during the Great Famine. In groups, students could then write their own songs on this subject. What do they miss about home? What is life like in America? Do they want to return to Ireland, and will they ever have enough money to do so?

CROSS-CURRICULAR LINKS

Dance link: although Irish solo dance is a highly specialised style, céilí dancing can be learned quickly to a basic level and is a fun activity for students. A céilí is a type of social gathering where everyone can join in with the dances, the steps to which are called out by the dance 'caller'. Professional dance callers exist in many parts of the UK, and can help your students to experience different types of Irish dance and the music that accompanies it. If an Irish dance caller isn't available, an English barndance can provide a very similar experience.

History link: Celtic music has a rich heritage and history that stretches back to the Iron Age. As part of this topic you could explore the long history of the Celts, or look at events in Irish history such as the Flight of the Earls and the Great Famine.

Art link: the ancient Celts had a very distinctive tradition of incorporating complex lattice designs and patterns into their art. Today, such designs have become fashionable as decoration for jewellery and clothing. You may wish to investigate the history of Celtic art and use this as a basis for creating your own designs.

RESOURCES

A great practical reason for studying Celtic music is that so many traditional tunes can be easily sourced from the internet, either as conventional Western notation, abc notation (a type of text-based notation popular with folk musicians) or MIDI files (which can be translated into notation in programs such as Sibelius and Logic). Three such websites that provide a bank of traditional tunes are www.thesession.org, www.tadpoletunes.com and www.cpmusic.com.

For further reading on Irish Celtic music, *The Rough Guide to Irish Music* (Rough Guides, 2001) is recommended.

INDIAN MUSIC

WHY TEACH INDIAN MUSIC?

Indian classical music has influenced Western popular and classical musicians from groups such as The Beatles, and compositional schools such as minimalism, to the West End musical. Due to its suitably 'exotic' nature and sound it has gained something of a reputation for being a quintessential type of world music, and it often crops up on music education syllabuses. It is also a challenging style of music to get to grips with, but it can be very rewarding to study and provides great opportunities to explore elements such as:

* Scales and modes (raga)
* Rhythm and rhythmic cycles (tala)
* Improvisation
* Ornamentation.

Indian classical music is divided into two fairly distinct traditions: Hindustani (north Indian) and Carnatic (south Indian). Due to certain influential musicians championing it, and the larger migration of north Indians, Hindustani music has gained the strongest foothold in the West and so it is the style this chapter will largely focus upon (with a brief look at the hugely popular Bollywood film industry as well).

AN INTRODUCTION TO INDIA

With an estimated population of over 1 billion people, India is the second most populous country in the world. It is geographically very diverse, from the Himalaya mountains at the top of the country, to the valleys and plains along the Ganges river system, to the Thar desert in the northwest. The climate divides broadly into three seasons: winter (November–February), summer (March–May) and monsoon (June–October), although the weather varies greatly depending on the region.

The most widely spoken language in India is **Hindi**, while English is the accepted business and administrative language. Many states also recognise their own official languages (such as Oriya in the state of Orissa, and Punjabi in the state of Punjab). The major religion is **Hinduism** (adhered to by about 80% of the population), followed by Islam (about 13%), with significant numbers of

Sikhs and Christians as well. India has a long and complex history that has led to much cultural and religious change. In order to put the classical music of India into a historical context, the following pages describe its origins and give a brief account of the country's history.

A BRIEF HISTORY

The roots of India can be traced back to the **Indus Valley civilisation** that thrived during 2600–1800 BC along the Indus River (which flows through the length of present-day Pakistan). This is thought to have been one of the three oldest civilisations in the world (the other two being Mesopotamia and Egypt). The civilisation went into decline around 1700 BC. Some archaeologists think this may have been due to natural causes (such as drought or flooding), while others believe the arrival of the first **Aryan** invaders played an important role.

The Aryans started to arrive in earnest during 1500 BC from central Asia, and came to occupy the whole of north India (conquering the indigenous Dravidians). Over the next 1000 years, India saw a succession of numerous warring kingdoms compete for territory and political power. During this time Brahmanism (a form of Hinduism) developed along with its caste system.

In the 4th century BC, under the leadership of King Chandragupta Maurya, the **Mauryan dynasty** took control of much of north India. His successor Asoka expanded the empire until it covered nearly the whole of India. After his death in 232 BC, the empire broke down into a system of smaller kingdoms and empires that came and went over the centuries. One that is worth mentioning is the **Gupta Empire**, which covered much of north India during the 4th to 6th centuries. This period is described as India's 'golden age', as successful administrative rule and relative political calm allowed for huge advancements in mathematics, astronomy, medicine and the arts.

Islam began to arrive in the 7th century, leading to the establishment of the Muslim **Mughal Empire** in the early 1500s, which at its peak in the 17th century covered most of India. During this period many Hindus were pressured into converting to Islam, and the opulent Taj Mahal was built (taking about 20 years to complete).

The **British East India Company** was founded in 1600 to trade with India, and with its growth Britain began to assert more and more political influence and power over India. By the 1850s the company controlled much of India.

However, widespread rebellions in 1857 led to the company's nationalisation, and its powers were transferred to the British Crown. Queen Victoria was proclaimed Empress of India in 1877, and this marked the beginning of the **British Raj**. British rule lasted until 1947 when, after pressure from Mohandas Gandhi and Jawaharlal Nehru, the British withdrew and India was given independence.

Origins of Indian classical music

Indian classical music is considered to be one of the world's oldest (continuous) musical traditions. As it has such an ancient history, certain details of its development are sketchy and disputed by academics. The earliest evidence lies in the *Sama Veda*: one of four sacred texts that exemplify principles and practices of the Vedic religion (from which Hinduism developed). The four *Vedas* were probably written between 1500 and 800 BC. The *Sama Veda* is a collection of hymns that, at the time, were chanted on a single note. Music and dance were considered divine in Vedic religion, able to communicate with and win the favour of the gods.

The *Ramayana* and *Mahabharata* – two Hindu epic poems thought to have been written around the 4th century BC – both make many references to musical practice. The *Ramayana*, for example, mentions instruments such as the venu (a bamboo flute) and mridanga (a type of drum). A number of the main characters practise music, including the evil king Ravana and the monkey king Sugriva. Both books provide very useful historical evidence of early Indian classical music, and their stories today feature heavily in the Indian classical arts.

The next known treatise to deal with music was the **Natyashastra**, a handbook for the performing arts which it is thought to have developed over a number of centuries (200 BC–AD 400). It provides great detail on stagecraft and classical dance, as well as musical instruments, performing technique and music theory. It was the most influential treatise on music for centuries, laying the foundations of the *raga* and *tala* systems of Indian classical music. The **Gupta dynasty** (see above) helped to build on these foundations by heavily patronising music and the dramatic arts.

Hindustani music develops

With the introduction of Islam to India (see above), Indian classical music began to split into two distinct types: **Hindustani** (north Indian) and **Carnatic** (south Indian). In the north of India, greatly influenced by Persian practice, music began to become more improvisatory (although still within the strict theoretical structures of raga and tala). Carnatic music on the other hand retained its fixed structure: a distinction that remains to this day.

A major figure in the 13th century was the poet and musician **Amir Khusrau**, who incorporated Persian and Arabic elements into Hindustani music. He is also thought to have brought the singing of *qawwali* (Sufi mystical poetry) and *ghazal* (an Arabic poetic form) into the accepted realms of Hindustani music.

As Hindustani music continued to develop its own improvisatory style, it found much patronage during the Mughal dynasty (see page 86). The emperor Akbar, in particular, was a strong supporter of the arts and his courts were rich with music and dance. Artists were recruited from a very wide area and the marriage of Indian and Persian musical practice thrived. The most famous of Akbar's court musicians was **Miyan Tansen**, who was considered to be so great a singer that he was attributed various supernatural gifts (such as the ability to bring rain or cause fire).

In the 20th century, Hindustani music theory was transformed by the work of **Vishnu Narayan Bhatkhande**. After many centuries of development and periods of disruption, Hindustani music was in array in terms of a formal, accepted theory of music. Bhatkhande performed extensive fieldwork throughout India and developed a system of classification that grouped ragas into *thats* (modes), addressing the problem of confusing relationships between ragas that resulted from numerous centuries of disjointed musicology. His treatise on Hindustani music is the most widely accepted of modern times.

The master-student tradition

Classical music is traditionally passed down in India through an ancient system of apprenticeship. This is known as the *guru-shishya* tradition ('guru' means 'master' and 'shishya' means 'disciple'), and is thought to date back to 2000 BC. It is the traditional way of learning many subjects in India such as religion, science, crafts and the arts. It is based upon a parent-child type of relationship where the master and student form a lifelong bond, with values such as respect, commitment and obedience at its core. In the case of music, a student traditionally goes to live in their teacher's house and in return for household duties and assistance, they are given musical instruction. Hindustani classical music is primarily an oral tradition: it relies on a huge volume of knowledge and technical ability being transmitted not through notated music but by patient demonstration and imitation.

Bollywood

The term 'Bollywood' refers to the Indian cinema industry that is based in Mumbai (previously known as Bombay) – the word is an amalgamation of 'Bombay' and 'Hollywood'. Bollywood films tend to include numerous songs (often about ten per film), which means that even non-Hindi-speaking audiences can enjoy the music and lavish production, giving the industry a national and lucrative appeal. Indeed, music can make or break a Bollywood film, and an important figure in a soundtrack's potential success is the **playback singer**.

Until the 1930s, actors sang their own songs in Bollywood films. But advancements in recording techniques and film technology led one production company (New Theatres) to introduce pre-recorded singing into their film *Dhoop Chaon* in 1935. This started the fashion for playback singers: vocalists who record the songs to a film separately, leaving the directors free to choose glamorous actors who don't need to be able to sing (but who instead mime the songs on set). Playback singers have since become artists in their own right, performing at concerts of *filmi sangeet* (film songs). Famous names include Mohammad Rafi, Asha Bosle and her sister Lata Mangeshkar.

Bollywood has made use of numerous styles of music over the decades, from light Indian classical in the early years to disco in the 1970s (Western-influenced pop styles are most common now). Bollywood songs dominate the Indian popular music charts, and form a major part of Indian music culture in general. For a typical example of a Bollywood song, listen to *Wada Na Tod*, sung by Lata Mangeshkar in YouTube video 'Indian 1: Bollywood'. You may already recognise this song from its inclusion in the 2004 American film *Eternal Sunshine of the Spotless Mind*.

> **Influences on Western music**
>
> Indian classical music has influenced a number of Western composers and musicians, including:
>
> * 20th-century composer Oliver Messiaen, who was the first Western composer to study the concept of tala seriously, and to incorporate Indian rhythms into his works (such as the *Turangalila-Symphonie*: see YouTube video 'Indian 2: Messiaen').
> * Minimalist composer Terry Riley, who studied with the Hindustani classical singer Pran Nath, and was greatly influenced by various theoretical elements of Hindustani music (listen for example to 'The Magic Knot Waltz' from *The Harp of New Albion*: see YouTube video 'Indian 3: Riley').
> * Jazz guitarist John Mclaughlin, who founded the Mahavishnu Orchestra: an experimental jazz-fusion group that displayed Indian influences (see for example YouTube video 'Indian 4: Mahavishnu').
> * George Harrison from the Beatles, who studied sitar with Ravi Shankar and did much to promote Indian music in the West. Listen for example to the very Indian-sounding 'Love You To' from the album *Revolver* (YouTube video 'Indian 5: Beatles').

VOCAL MUSIC

Hindustani classical music should be understood primarily as a vocal tradition, based around the singing of religious or romantic poetry. While instrumental music is of no lesser importance (and more frequently seen on the international music circuit), it developed out of the vocal raga tradition (and instruments were designed according to this). It is essentially vocal music without the voice.

A few of the most prominent styles of Hindustani classical vocal music are briefly described below.

Qawwali

Qawwali is the singing of Sufi (Islamic mystic) hymns that utilise the Hindustani music system. It is often credited to the 13th-century Sufi musician Amir Khusrau (see page 88), but probably existed in some form before that. In contrast to orthodox Islam, which does not permit the use of music for worship, Sufi Islam uses music as a fundamental spiritual vehicle.

Qawwali is usually performed by one or two lead *qawwals* (qawwali singers), who are accompanied by a small male chorus, harmoniums and a frenetic style of tabla playing. The music is intended to instil a highly charged emotional state in the listener, which is achieved through the virtuosic vocal style and repetitive, hypnotic tabla playing. Today, Pakistan has a particularly strong qawwali tradition with revered singers such as The Sabri Bothers, Abida Parveen and Nusrat Fateh Ali Khan (who performs in YouTube video 'Indian 6: qawwali').

Dhrupad

Dhrupad is one of the oldest styles of vocal singing in Hindustani classical music, thought to have developed in the 15th and 16th centuries. It is an austere, slow moving and highly structured form of singing that has largely fallen out of favour today. However, it influenced the development of the much more popular khyal (see below) and played an important part in establishing the modern alap-jor-jhala-gat structure. It is typically accompanied by two tanpuras and a single barrel-shaped drum known as the pakhawaj (the predecessor to the tabla). See YouTube video 'Indian 7: dhrupad' for an example of this style of singing.

Khyal

Khyal (Hindi for 'idea' or 'imagination') rose to prominence in the 18th century – just as the performance of dhrupad was going into decline – and is today one of the most popular forms of Hindustani classical vocal music. Khyal is a freer style of singing that relies more upon improvisation and thus allows room for greater displays of virtuosity.

Khyal singing is today accompanied by tanpura, harmonium and tabla. The style generally has a very short alap section (if there is one at all), focusing instead on the pre-composed sections of sung poetry and the improvisations, both in slow and fast talas. Famous exponents of this style include Kishori Amonkar, Shruti Sadolikar and Pandit Jasraj. Watch YouTube video 'Indian 8: khyal' for an example of khyal singing.

INSTRUMENTATION

The following section briefly describes some of the most important instruments in Hindustani classical music.

Sitar: perhaps the most prominent modern Hindustani classical instrument, the sitar has been made famous globally by the musician Ravi Shankar. It is a long-necked lute that typically has about 20 strings: three or four melody strings, three or four drone strings and around 13 sympathetic strings. These sympathetic strings run underneath the frets and resonate in sympathy with the main strings (so when a melody note is played, the corresponding sympathetic string will vibrate). The resulting effect contributes to the sitar's rich, shimmering sound. YouTube video 'Indian 9: sitar' is a performance by the renowned Ravi Shankar with his daughter Anoushka Shankar.

Bansuri: a transverse flute, typically made of bamboo, with six or seven finger holes. It is culturally significant in that it is the instrument associated with the Hindu god Krishna, who is often portrayed in a pastoral setting (as he was raised by a cowherd family) playing the flute. Until relatively recently it was solely a folk instrument, and struggled to be considered capable of the technical demands and subtleties of classical music. The 20th-century bansuri master Panalal Ghosh did much to raise its status, and it is now an accepted instrument in the classical world. One of its best known exponents internationally is Hariprasad Chaurasia, who performs in YouTube video 'Indian 10: bansuri'.

Tanpura: a lute that is similar in construction to the sitar, with a gourd resonator and a long wooden neck. It typically has four strings (often tuned to the tonic and dominant) that are used to play a drone. Like the sitar, its curved bridge allows the strings to resonate with harmonics.

Harmonium: a European addition to Indian music, the harmonium was brought to the country in the 19th century by Christian missionaries. The portable hand-pumped version quickly became more popular than the pedal harmonium – primarily because it suited the practice of sitting on the floor to perform – and today it is a prominent instrument in Indian classical music. The bellows are pumped with one hand while the other hand plays a melody on the small piano keyboard; Indian harmoniums can also produce their own drones. See YouTube video 'Indian 11: harmonium' for a demonstration of this instrument.

Tabla: the most commonly used percussion instrument in Hindustani classical music. It consists of a pair of hand drums: a small right-hand drum usually made of wood (the 'daya' or 'tabla'), and a slightly larger left-hand drum typically made of metal (the 'baya'). One of the most distinctive features of the tabla is the large black spot in the centre of each drum head, made from a type of rice paste mixed with iron shavings. They help to create the characteristic bell-like timbre of the drum.

One of the most internationally famous tabla players is Allah Rakha, who performed with Ravi Shankar for many years. He demonstrates the different sounds the tabla can produce in YouTube video 'Indian 12: tabla'.

Dhol: The dhol is a double-headed, barrel-shaped drum that is hung over the shoulder with a leather strap. It is played with two sticks, one thin and straight for the higher-pitched treble head, and one hooked and chunky for the lower-pitched bass head. This drum is traditionally used to accompany folk dances at weddings and festivals. It is generally associated with Punjabi culture, but has spread to other parts of India and features frequently in Bollywood films. See YouTube video 'Indian 13: dhol' for a demonstration of this drum.

CHARACTERISTIC FEATURES OF THE STYLE

Hindustani music is organised around three basic principles: the **raga** (melodic system), **tala** (rhythmic cycle) and an accompanying **drone**. Let us consider each in turn.

Raga

The term 'raga' derives from a Sanskrit word meaning 'to colour'. The Hindi/Urdu form of the word is 'rag' but the two spellings are commonly interchangeable. The basic principle of raga performance is that it instils a certain feeling or mood (*rasa*) in the listener. According to the ancient *Natyashastra* treatise, there are nine rasa from which all emotions are derived.

These are as follows:

Rasa	Emotion
Shringara	Love/attraction
Hasya	Joy/humour
Adbhuta	Wonder/mystery
Shanta	Peace
Raudra	Anger/rage
Veera	Courage/pride
Karuna	Sadness/compassion
Bhayanaka	Fear
Vibhatsa	Disgust/dissatisfaction

Although commonly thought of as a type of mode or scale, the term raga refers to much more than this. The following are some of its main features:

* It has a certain mood (rasa).
* It is intended to be performed at a certain time of day (e.g. raga Desh is a late evening raga) or season of the year (e.g. raga Megh is a monsoon raga).
* It must have at least five notes (*swaras*).
* It has an ascending pattern (*arohana*) that may be different from the descending pattern (*avarohana*).
* It has a dominant note (*vadi*) and a secondary dominant note (*samvadi*) – usually a 4th or 5th apart – that must be emphasised in performance.
* It may have certain notes that must be ornamented.
* It has certain melodic catchphrases (*pakad*).

In combination these variables give each raga a particular character and mood, providing a type of framework that forms the basis for a melodic performance.

As well as being associated with a specific time or season, a few ragas are believed to have magical or medicinal powers. For example, it is said that when Emperor Akbar's court musician Miyan Tansen performed raga Dipak, he could cause fire to break out. For this reason, some Indian musicians are wary of this raga today.

Notes and tuning

Like Western music, Indian classical music is based upon seven notes (swaras) that can be natural (*shuddh*), flat (*komal*) or sharp (*tivra*), creating 12 basic pitches within the octave. The degrees of the scale are named according to the *sargam* system, which is similar to the sol-fa system used in the West:

Degree	1	2	3	4	5	6	7	8
Sargam	Sa	Re	Ga	Ma	Pa	Dha	Ni	Sa
Sol-fa	Do	Re	Mi	Fa	So	La	Ti	Do

It is worth noting that Indian classical music hasn't adopted the fixed, equal-temperament tuning of the West but uses the natural harmonic series for its intonation instead (known as 'just intonation'). This means that the exact frequency of each note is determined by the intervals of the scale it is being used in, rather than having an absolute frequency regardless of the context (such as 440 Hz for an A).

In performance, this means that the first note of the raga (*sa*) is fixed at a point that suits the singer's mid range, so they can reach the middle, lower and higher octaves comfortably. Instruments generally follow this principle as well, and within the confines of their construction they tune to a good-sounding 'sa' rather than an A at 440 Hz.

Ornamentation

There are various types of ornaments (*alankar*) used to decorate the notes of a raga. Probably the most characteristic ornament is the **pitch bend** (*meend*): a slide between two notes. It was firstly a vocal technique, and instruments were developed specifically so they could achieve the same effect (which, for example, led to the curved frets on the sitar). Ornamentation is hugely important in Hindustani classical music and it is rare for any one note to stand alone, without being connected to its preceding or succeeding note in some way through ornamentation.

Comparing two raga

In order to illustrate some of these features, let's examine two common ragas and compare their characteristics.

Raga Desh:

Raga Bhoopali:

Features	Raga Desh	Raga Bhoopali
Mood	Romantic	Devotional
Performance time	Evening	Evening
Number of notes	5 ascending/7 descending	5 ascending + descending
Ascent/descent	Different	Same
Dominant note	Re	Ga
Secondary note	Pa	Dha

From the notations and the table above we can see that these two raga differ in a number of ways. This illustrates how any particular raga creates its own mood and character by using a unique combination of melodic and performance variables. Try singing or playing up and down the notes of the two raga above and improvising around them: you should quickly get a basic sense of their different characters. You can watch YouTube videos 'Indian 14: raga Desh' and 'Indian 15: raga Bhoopali' to see performances of these two ragas.

Drone

The drone is a vital part of Hindustani music, providing a tonal reference point for the notes of the raga. Whereas Western music is based upon the harmonisation of a melody line with chords that change frequently, Hindustani music deeply explores the expressive potential of one set of notes over a continuous drone.

Drones can be provided in a number of ways. For vocal music, the tanpura (see page 92) plays a drone that frequently consists of the tonic (sa) and the dominant (pa). Some instruments can create their own drone in addition to playing the melody (such as the sitar), although it is standard practice to include a dedicated 'drone' instrument in the ensemble as well.

Indian-made harmoniums (see page 92) have drone stops that provide constant droning pitches, and the shruti box (essentially a harmonium with no keyboard) is designed to do the same. In more recent times, electronic shruti boxes have become popular as they are highly portable and relatively cheap.

Tala

Rhythm in Hindustani music is organised around the concept of 'tala'. This refers to a constantly repeating cycle of a set number (and pattern) of beats. It provides the rhythmic framework for a performance (in a similar way to how the raga provides the melodic framework). The tala is usually elaborated by the tabla player, who commonly enters a piece after the notes of the raga have been explored by the vocalist or instrumentalist in a free rhythm (see page 98).

Although there are hundreds of different talas in Hindustani classical music, today there are only about 15 in common use. These include Tintal (16 beats), Jhaptal (10 beats), Rupak tala (7 beats) and Dadra tala (6 beats). The following list outlines the main features of the tala.

* Each tala has a fixed number of beats (*matras*).
* Each tala subdivides into a number of sections (*vibhags*), with a fixed number of beats in each (similar to the concept of the bar in Western music, although vibhags are not always of equal lengths).
* The first beat in each vibhag may be accented to a greater or lesser extent, and these accents can be represented visually by a series of claps (*tali*) and hand waves (*khali*). A clap indicates a stronger

beat, while a hand wave indicates a weaker beat. This helps to give a structure to the tala, and also allows musicians to communicate with each other during a performance.

* The first beat of the cycle (*sam*) is the most important and receives the strongest emphasis (being represented with a clap according to the system above).
* Each tala has a specific pattern of drum strokes (*bols*), which are represented with different syllables (such as 'dha' and 'tin'). See YouTube video 'Indian 16: bols' for a demonstration of the different drum strokes.
* Talas can be performed at a number of different speeds, ranging from 'very slow' (*ati vilambit*) to 'very fast' (*ati drut*).
* Each repetition of a cycle is known as an *avartan*.

One of the most common talas is Tintal, a 16-beat cycle that is split into four vibhags of four beats each:

Beat	1 (clap)	2	3	4	5 (clap)	6	7	8
Drum strokes	Dha	Dhin	Dhin	Dha	Dha	Dhin	Dhin	Dha
Beat	9 (wave)	10	11	12	13 (clap)	14	15	16
Drum strokes	Dha	Tin	Tin	Ta	Ta	Dhin	Dhin	Dha

YouTube video 'Indian 17: Tintal' is an example of a tabla solo in Tintal.

Structure

A performance of a raga may take a variety of different structures, but a format that has become popular in recent years is the 'alap–jor–jhala–gat' structure. This consists of the following sections:

Section	Sub-section	Typical features
Alap		Very slow/free rhythm. The soloist improvises around the notes of the raga, presenting them systematically and establishing the rasa. Accompanied only by a drone.
Jor		The soloist continues to explore/improvise around the raga but a regular pulse is introduced.

Jhala		More exploration/improvisation but with faster notes to a regular pulse.
Gat	Gat	The soloist stops improvising and instead performs a fixed composition. The tabla enters, playing the chosen tala.
	Improvisations	After the gat has been presented the soloist begins to improvise (still strictly within the rules of the raga).
	Returns to the gat	After a period of improvisation the soloist returns to the gat, and this alternation continues throughout the performance.
	Tabla solo	In some performances, the soloist permits the tabla player to take a solo, allowing them to demonstrate their virtuosity.
	Gat/improvisation	The music gradually increases in pace as the soloist continues to improvise and make references back to the gat.
	Jugalbandi	The soloist and tabla player engage in fast, virtuosic question-and-answer melodic interplay.
	Tihai	At a very fast pace, the soloist and tabla play a thrice repeated phrase in unison (the 'tihai') that leads them to finish on the 'sam' (the first beat of the cycle).

In a traditional setting it is not unusual for a raga performance to last for over an hour, although shorter performances are becoming more common in order to accommodate international tastes. A comparatively short performance is given by the famous sitar player Ravi Shankar in YouTube video 'Indian 18: Shankar', which is a sort of potted version of the structure above, and a good introduction to standard performance practice.

LISTENING EXAMPLE

'Mohe Panghat Pe' is a Bollywood song in a light classical style from the film *Mughal-e-Azam* ('Greatest of the Mughals') released in 1960. The film is one of the biggest box-office successes in the history of Bollywood. It tells the story of the young Mughal Prince Salim (son of Emperor Akbar) and his tragic love affair with the court dancer Anarkali. The film is a great introduction to Hindustani music in a light classical style.

'Mohe Panghat Pe' is in the style of a Hindu *bhajan* (hymn) that tells the story of Krishna and his playful teasing of a girl at a well. This is a common theme in Hindu mythology and there is much poetry written about Krishna's mischievousness.

The original film was in black-and-white with a few colour scenes. In 2004 the film was re-released in colour (with a re-recorded soundtrack). You can watch the scene that contains the song 'Mohe Panghat Pe' from the 2004 version in YouTube video 'Indian 19: Mughal-e-Azam'. In this scene, Anarkali and a group of female dancers and musicians are providing entertainment for the royal court. The song is also available on the album *Mughal-e-Azam Deluxe Version* (which is the version the timeline below is based on). 'Mohe Panghat Pe' was composed in raga Gara, the notes of which are:

| Sa | Ga | Ma | Pa | Ni | Sa | | Sa | Ni | Dha | Pa | Ma | Ga | Re | Ga | Re | Sa |

Introduction/alap	
0:00	Instrumental introduction played by sitars, with an accompanying drone (tanpura and keyboard). Tabla play a fast Tintal (16-beat cycle), and the ghungroo (metal bells) emphasise the beat.
0:14	A tihai is played to end the introduction (see page 99).
0:23	Short alap-style vocal section on the notes of raga Gara to the vocable 'ah'. Tanpura and keyboard drone continue.
0:35	Bansuri interlude (just played by one at first before others join in at 0:41).
Verse 1	
0:44	Tabla plays an introductory flourish and a new 6-beat tala (Dadra) begins.
0:45	Vocal song begins. Tabla continues to play the tala with decorative improvisations. Drone moves from the tonic to seventh at points. Piano vamps chords and strings double the vocal line. *Mohe Panghat Pe Nandlal Chhed Gayo Re* Krishna teased me at the well *Mori Najuk Kalaiyaa Marod Gayo Re* He twisted my delicate wrist
1:16	Female chorus repeats the first line above.
1:27	Sitars play an instrumental interlude.

Verse 2	
1:38	Soloist begins the second stanza, with the soloist and chorus alternating the following phrase: *Kankari Mohe Maari Gagariya Phod Daali* He cast a pebble at my pitcher and broke it
2:05	Soloist starts the next line with a short vocal *tan* (a rapid series of improvised notes) to the vocable 'ah', before continuning with: *Mori Saree Anari Bhigoyi Gayo Re* My garment (sari) was dripping wet
2:25	Female chorus repeats the first line of the song.
2:37	Bansuris play an instrumental interlude.
Verse 3	
2:47	Soloist continues with the next line, which is repeated between the soloist and chorus: *Nayno Se Jadoo Kiya Jiyara Moh Liya* He cast a magic glance and won my heart
3:14	Another short tan leads into: *Mora Ghoongat Najariya Se Khol Gayo Re* With his glance, he pierced my veil *Mohe Panghat Pe* (short tans) *Mohe Panghat Pe* (short tans) *Mohe Panghat Pe Nandlal Chhed Gayo Re* Krishna teased me at the well
3:50	Sitars and bansuris play a short jugalbandi (question and answer) section ending with a final unison phrase.

After listening to this song, your students could test their understanding of it with the following questions:

1. What is the first melody instrument heard in the introduction? (Sitar)
2. When the singer first enters, what is happening in the accompaniment? (Drone only: tabla, sitar and ghungroo drop out)
3. Where in the song can you hear a tihai? (0:14 at the end of the instrumental introduction)

4. When the lyrics of the song begin at 0:45, the tabla starts to play a 6-beat cycle called Dadra tala. Listen closely to the tabla accompaniment: which of the following basic rhythms is it playing?

(The second one)

5. The solo vocalist occasionally starts a line with a short tan. What is a tan? (A rapid series of improvised notes/a type of ornamentation)
6. When the sitars play their instrumental interlude at 1:27, how they are moving between the notes? (With slides/pitch bends)
7. You can hear a drone throughout this song. What is a drone? (A sustained note that is held in one part while a melody is heard above it)
8. This song is sung by the famous playback singer Lata Mangeshkar. What can you say about her vocal style? (It is melismatic/ornamental, with a soft vocal tone)

PERFORMING

A simple piece in an 'Indian' style is available to download from the book website, which you can use as the basis for a performance project. It makes use of some of the characteristic features of Indian classical music mentioned earlier in the chapter. The piece uses the notes of raga Bhoopali (see page 96) and is set in Tintal (see page 98). It begins with a short alap in which the catchphrases of the raga are heard. This is followed by a series of vocal exercises in Tintal, which are presented in a jugalbandi (question-and-answer) style. The spoken tabla part includes the basic tala and a short solo in the middle.

To perform this piece you could divide your class into four groups: two to sing the vocal lines, one to speak/play the tabla part, and one to play the drone that continues throughout (this can be played on any instrument that sustains well).

COMPOSING

Over the years, Bollywood has used many styles of music in its films from Indian classical to disco and modern dance music. Using raga Bhoopali (or another raga of their choice), your students could write their own Bollywood song that follows these rules:

* Write two to three verses on the theme of missing someone that you love, and a one-line refrain to be repeated after each verse.
* Only use the notes of your chosen raga for the melody, which will help to give it an 'Indian' sound.
* Write an accompaniment that displays some sort of 'Indian' influence. This could be through the addition of a tabla part (in Tintal perhaps?) or a tonic drone.

CROSS-CURRICULAR LINKS

Religious Education link: studying the music of India provides an ideal opportunity to explore a number of the world's major faith groups. Hinduism, Islam, Sikhism, Buddhism and Christianity are all represented in India. In particular, the two Hindu epic poems (the *Mahabharata* and *Ramayana*) have strong links to Hindustani classical music.

Art link: India has a rich tradition of Hindu, Sikh and Muslim art, architecture and textiles. You may like to explore topics such as the depiction of Hindu gods, Muslim calligraphic art or Mughal architecture (such as the Taj Mahal).

Film link: the history of Bollywood – in particular, the types of themes, stories and conventions that have been in vogue over the decades – can be very interesting to study. Likewise the 2008 British film *Slumdog Millionaire* is worth investigating, with its soundtrack by the Indian composer Allah Rakha Rahman that fuses Indian classical music with hip-hop, electronica and other contemporary styles.

RESOURCES

Although Indian classical music is perhaps one of the hardest world-music styles to learn and perform in the classroom, there are nonetheless a number of organisations in the UK that can provide Indian-themed workshops for schools, which can help to demystify the music for your students. Otherwise, the following resources may be of help:

Books and CDs

* *Indian Music for the Classroom* by Natalie Sarrazin (Rowman & Littlefield Education, 2008): specifically designed for school use, this book includes lesson activities, transcriptions and information about a variety of Indian styles.
* *Music in North India* by George E. Ruckert (Oxford University Press, 2004): a short book that provides a good introduction to Hindustani classical music, accompanied by a CD.
* 'Rough Guide' CDs such as *The Rough Guide to the Music of India*, *The Rough Guide to Ravi Shankar* and *The Rough Guide to Bollywood*: good compilation CDS that cover a variety of Indian styles and musicians.

Websites

The websites www.chandrakantha.com and www.soundofindia.com both provide useful information about Indian music. The Wesleyan University 'Virtual Instrument Museum' website (http://learningobjects.wesleyan.edu/vim/) has images, videos and information about a number of Indian instruments.

JAVANESE GAMELAN

WHY TEACH GAMELAN?

A gamelan is an ensemble of tuned-percussion instruments that is found throughout Indonesia and Malaysia. The basic ensemble consists of various metallophones, gongs and drums; flutes, string instruments and voices are often added as well. Gamelan ensembles come in a number of different varieties, from the reserved, stately performances of the royal palaces in Central Java, to the energetic and virtuosic gamelan gong kebyar in Bali. Over the last few decades the gamelan music of Central Java and Bali, in particular, has become popular outside of Indonesia. This chapter focuses on Central Javanese gamelan, which is arguably the best-known gamelan style in the West and, as a result, is well served in terms of literature and resources.

Perhaps the main reason why gamelan has become popular in UK schools is the fact that it is so accessible as a practical activity. The instruments are easy to play and the melodies are usually short and repetitive. In addition, the fact that the music is performed without a conductor or any sort of notation means that players really have to listen to each other, which makes gamelan a brilliant genre for developing ensemble skills.

There are other reasons why you might like to teach gamelan:

* It is a great medium through which to study pentatonic scales and heterophonic textures
* It can provide students with an insight into the rich cultural heritage of southeast Asia
* The fairly rigid structure of the music means that it can lead to a simple, straightforward composition project.

AN INTRODUCTION TO INDONESIA

Indonesia is made up of over **17,000 islands**, around 6,000 of which are inhabited, making it the largest archipelago in the world. Four of the five biggest islands in Indonesia are known collectively as the **Greater Sunda** group, which includes Borneo, Sumatra, Sulawesi and Java.

Java is a long, thin and densely populated island: it has an area similar to the size of England, but a population that is more than twice as large (138 million compared to England's 53 million). Most of these people are crammed into the cities around the exterior of the island (such as **Jakarta** on the northwest coast, which is the capital of both Java and Indonesia). The interior, in contrast, largely consists of a string of volcanic mountains and swathes of rice fields.

Java is divided into **four provinces**: Banten, East Java, Central Java and West Java. These four provinces are quite culturally distinct from one another, with different musical traditions and even different languages. (The main language in Central and East Java is **Javanese**, while in West Java the dominant language is Sundanese. Most people, however, also speak Indonesian as a second language – which is the official language of Indonesia). Central Javanese gamelan, for example, shouldn't be confused with West Javanese gamelan, which is a different type of ensemble that plays a contrasting body of music.

As an archipelago, Indonesia has been subjected to many outside influences through **maritime trade**. From the 1st to 7th centuries, for example, trade with India led to the Hindu and Buddhist faiths being established in Indonesia. From around the 13th century, through the influence of Arab traders and missionaries, **Islam** began to spread, and by the end of the 16th century it had become the predominant religion. Today, almost 90% of the population is Muslim.

GAMELAN MUSIC

It is commonly thought that gamelan music first developed in **Central Java** and then spread to other parts of the island, Bali and the rest of the region. Although a definitive history of its origins remain elusive, early evidence can be found in the stone carvings at the Borobudur Buddhist temple in Central Java, which dates back to the **9th century**. These carvings depict a number of instruments such as double-headed drums, xylophones and flutes.

The earliest form of the gamelan still in existence today is the **gamelan munggang**, which consists of three-tone gongs and gong chimes. It is thought to date from the 12th century. To begin with, gamelan ensembles were divided into two different styles: loud and soft. The loud ensembles (which included the more penetrating metallophones and drums) were used for outdoor religious ceremonies and processions. The soft ensembles (which included wooden xylophones, flutes and quieter metallophones) were used indoors, probably to accompany the singing of Javanese poetry. These two types of ensemble were combined in the **17th century** to create the larger ensemble used today.

Since the ensemble first developed, the main centres of gamelan music in Central Java have been the **royal courts** (*kraton*). Today there are four royal courts in Central Java: two in the city of Yogyakarta (or Jogja) and two in the city of Surakarta (or Solo). These courts are thriving cultural institutions, each housing a number of different gamelan that are used on a regular basis for ceremonies and festivities.

Gamelan music is also heard widely outside of the courts. Performances generally accompany special occasions or religious ceremonies: weddings, anniversaries, births, festivals and other important events usually include a gamelan performance. Radio performances are very common on Radio Republik Indonesia, as are performances in concert halls and tourist locations. Many villages will also own a gamelan, although they are often not as large or refined as the stately court ensembles.

YouTube videos 'Gamelan 1: Javanese 1' and 'Gamelan 2: Javanese 2' are typical performances from Central Java that will give you an introduction to this style of music.

Shadow-puppet theatre

Gamelan music is frequently used to accompany shadow-puppet theatre (***wayang kulit***). This is extremely popular and the performances can draw very large crowds. The plays are usually based on stories from two Hindu epic poems: the *Mahabharata* and *Ramayana*.

The play itself is performed by a highly respected ***dhalang*** (master puppeteer). The dhalang's role is very demanding in that it involves operating the puppets against a shadow screen; narrating and providing the dialogue; engaging in quick-witted banter with the audience; and directing the gamelan musicians. Performances are traditionally held during the night and can last for up to nine hours – so the dhalang also needs to have immense powers of concentration! – although in recent times, shorter plays have developed as well. Wayang kulit is as much a social gathering as a piece of theatre, and during the performance the audience tends to come and go, take refreshments, chat and sleep.

YouTube video 'Gamelan 3: wayang 1' explains more about the practice of wayang kulit, while 'Gamelan 4: wayang 2' is an excerpt from a performance.

Influences on Western music

In 1889, Paris celebrated the centenary of the French Revolution with an *Exposition Universelle*. This world fair – which showcased the brand new Eiffel Tower – exhibited a number of cultural groups from around the world, including a Javanese gamelan. Claude Debussy and Erik Satie both visited the fair, and they became fascinated with the tuning and textures of the gamelan. Their experience inspired such pieces as Debussy's 'Pagodas' from *Estampes* (which features pentatonic scales and gamelan-like textures: see YouTube video 'Gamelan 5: Debussy'), and Satie's *Gnossiennes* (with their 'exotic' flavour: see YouTube video 'Gamelan 6: Satie').

The influence of gamelan music has since extended into the 20th century: minimalist composers such as Steve Reich and Philip Glass, for example, have been inspired by the repetition and interlocking textures found in gamelan music. Popular musicians such as Mike Oldfield and King Crimson have also been influenced by it.

INSTRUMENTATION

It can take highly skilled blacksmiths many weeks to make a complete gamelan: YouTube video 'Gamelan 7: making instruments' will give you a short taster of the work involved. The more expensive gamelan are made from bronze, while cheaper alternatives use iron or brass.

Gamelan are often treated with great respect and humility. The older gamelan in the royal courts, for example, are usually considered to be sacred; they are given individual names (such as 'Fountain of Honey' or 'Prosperous Realm'), and receive regular offerings of flowers, incense and food. Musicians always remove their shoes to play gamelan and usually avoid stepping over the instruments. For some this is primarily just a matter of courtesy – in the same way that you wouldn't want to step over a room full of orchestral instruments lying on the floor – but for others it is a way of not offending the spirits in the gamelan itself.

The following section gives a brief description of the most important instruments in a Central Javanese gamelan.

Metallophones

These refer to the xylophone-like instruments that usually play the core melody (the *balungan*) from which all of the other parts are derived. There are a few different varieties, including:

* The **saron** instruments: these each have six to seven thick bronze keys that are suspended over a wooden resonating case. There are three different sizes: the largest (and lowest-pitched) is the **saron demung**; the **saron barung** sounds an octave higher than the demung; and the **saron panerus** (also known as the **peking**) sounds an octave higher still. The first two of these instruments usually just play the core melody, while the peking typically decorates it.
* The **gender** instruments: these are similar to the saron, but their keys are thinner and suspended over resonating tubes (as with a vibraphone), resulting in a softer sound. The **gender panerus** sounds an octave higher than the **gender barung**; both of these instruments tend to embellish the core melody. The **slenthem** is the lowest-pitched metallophone and usually plays the basic version of the balungan.

All of the metallophones require a slightly tricky damping technique, where you damp the previous note as you play the next one. For the sarons, this requires your non-playing hand to shadow your playing hand, pinching the edge of one key as you strike the next one. For the gender panerus and barung, as both hands are already holding mallets, the player has to damp with their wrists – a difficult skill to master! YouTube videos 'Gamelan 8: damping 1' and 'Gamelan 9: damping 2' demonstrate these playing techniques.

Gongs

A gamelan ensemble includes two types of gongs: smaller 'pot' gongs and larger hanging gongs. The most important of the 'pot' gongs are:

* The **bonang**: this instrument consists of 10 to 12 small gongs the sit horizontally in a wooden rack. There are two different sizes: the **bonang panerus** sounds an octave higher than the **bonang barung**. These instruments usually embellish the melody. You can see a close-up of them being played in YouTube video 'Gamelan 10: bonang'.

* The **kenong**: this is similar to the bonang, but the gongs are a little larger and there are fewer of them. This instrument punctuates the melody by playing on certain beats of the cycle.

There are three different types of hanging gong:

* The **gong ageng**: this is the largest hanging gong and arguably the most important instrument in the whole ensemble. It is a very heavy and low-sounding gong, which is generally played on the last beat of the cycle. All of the other players orientate themselves, musically speaking, to the gong ageng.
* The **suwukan**: a medium-sized gong that punctuates the cycle.
* The **kempul**: a set of smaller hanging gongs that, like the suwukan, are used to punctuate the cycle.

Drums

A gamelan ensemble is led by the drummer, who plays a number of important roles in a performance. By incorporating a system of rhythmic signals into their part, the drummer can control and vary the tempo and structure of a piece. If the ensemble is accompanying dancers or actors, the drummer acts as an important link between all of the performers, making sure that the music closely follows the action happening on stage.

The main type of drum is the **kendhang**: a double-headed, barrel-shaped drum that is played with the hands. Like the other instruments in the gamelan, the kendhang comes in a variety of different sizes (such as the larger kendhang ageng and smaller kendhang ketipung); they are usually played in pairs. YouTube video 'Gamelan 11: kendhang' provides a demonstration of this instrument.

Others

There are a few other melody instruments that might be included in the ensemble, such as:

* The **rebab**: a two-stringed fiddle with a small, heart-shaped body and a thin wooden neck. It is played vertically (similar to the much larger cello). It typically plays a more lyrical, ornamented version of the balungan. (See for example YouTube video 'Gamelan 12: rebab'.)

* The **suling**: a small bamboo flute that is also played vertically. Despite its size it can generate quite a loud, piercing sound, and tends to improvise around the balungan. (YouTube video 'Gamelan 13: suling' features a rebab and suling at the start of the piece.)
* The **gambang**: much like a xylophone, with around 20 thin wooden keys that sit over a wooden resonating case. It usually embellishes the balungan with fast melodic patterns. (See for example YouTube video 'Gamelan 14: gambang'.)

Voices

Central Javanese gamelan are often accompanied by either a male chorus (the *gerong*) or solo female singers (known as *sinden*). The gerong will usually sing pre-composed melodies that are settings of Javanese poetry, such as in YouTube video 'Gamelan 15: gerong'. In contrast, solo female singers tend to improvise over the balungan and have a greater amount of rhythmic freedom. In this sense, their role is similar to the rebab or suling, floating above the regulated pulsing of the other gamelan instruments (see YouTube video 'Gamelan 16: sinden').

CHARACTERISTIC FEATURES OF THE STYLE

Gamelan music can seem a little impenetrable when you first approach it, but in fact the music generally adheres to quite fixed structures and principles, which are simple enough to comprehend once you have seen how they work in practice. The following section will help you to understand gamelan music better by explaining its main features and principles.

Tuning systems

There are two different tuning systems (or scales) used in Central Javanese gamelan: slendro and pelog. **Slendro** is a pentatonic scale in which each interval is roughly equidistant: about 1¼ tones apart. It is impossible to translate this scale exactly into Western notation, but an approximation is:

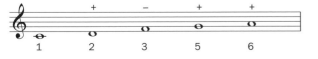

Pelog is a heptatonic scale in which the intervals vary in size, and can be likened to the following Western pitches:

Although the pelog scale is heptatonic, the majority of pieces only use five of the seven pitches available, which means that in practice nearly all gamelan music is pentatonic. YouTube video 'Gamelan 17: tuning' explains and demonstrates the differences between the two types of scale in more detail.

The pitches given above are rough approximations: gamelan do not adhere to a standardised tuning system, and no two gamelan are tuned exactly the same (which means that instruments are never swapped between ensembles). The two scales also require two different sets of instruments, so if an ensemble wants to play pieces in both pelog and slendro, their gamelan will need to include two of each instrument: one tuned in slendro and one in pelog.

You may have noticed that the pitches in the scales above are numbered. These refer to a form of **cipher notation** that has been developed for gamelan music, which is used to act as a memory aid more than anything else (gamelan is primarily an oral tradition). Each note in the scale is given a number, and the numbers are used to notate the core melody.

Pathet

Melody in gamelan music is organised according to the concept of *pathet*, which is similar to the Indian concept of raga (see page 93). For each pathet, different notes of the slendro or pelog scale are given particular emphasis, and stressed at more important points in the music (such as at the end of a cycle). The different pathets are associated with different moods and emotions, similar to Indian raga. For Central Javanese gamelan there are traditionally six pathet: three each for pelog and slendro tunings. In the slendro scale, for example, pathet *sanga* stresses pitches 5 and 1 (while tending to avoid pitch 3), whereas pathet *manyura* stresses pitches 6 and 2 (while tending to avoid pitch 5).

Irama

Irama is a concept that essentially defines the melodic density of the music. It refers to the ratio of notes played by the fast, elaborating instruments compared to the balungan. There are five different irama, and the best way to distinguish between them is to look at how many notes the peking plays for each note of the balungan:

Irama	No. of peking notes per balungan note	Balungan speed
Lancar	1	Fast
Tangung	2	↓
Dadi	4	↓
Wilet	8	↓
Rangkep	16	Slow

The slower the irama, the slower the balungan, and the more space there is for melodic elaboration. As a result, the surface of the music can often sound busier in a slower irama, while in contrast the punctuating instruments are much more spaced out.

The concept of irama is easier to understand in practice. For a demonstration of how it works, visit the website 'gamelan mecanique' at www.citedelamusique. fr/gamelan/shock.html. This is an interactive gamelan that allows you to mute different instruments to work out what's going on in the music. There are two pieces played on a Central Javanese gamelan; you can listen to the second one, *Ladrang*, in two different irama.

It is worth noting that irama is not the same as tempo (*laya*), as any particular irama can be performed at different speeds. The subtle changing between different irama and tempi within a performance is one of the things that can make the music so interesting.

The balungan

Much gamelan music is organised around a **core melody** called the balungan. This is usually quite short – often a multiple of 8 beats long – and simply repeated as an ostinato by the larger sarons. The notes of this melody are frequently all of the same length, as in the balungan for the piece *Lancaran*:

The balungan forms the backbone of the piece from which all of the other players derive their parts. Most balungan have a short instrumental introduction called a *buka*.

Colotomic structure

The phrase 'colotomic structure' is basically used to describe the way that gamelan music can be divided into smaller and smaller units of time.

* The longest unit of time – one cycle of the core melody (called a **gongan**) – is marked by a stroke on the gong ageng.
* The other hanging gongs and the kenong are often used to divide the gongan into halves or quarters.
* The balungan then marks every minim or crotchet beat.
* The saron and bonang divide the music further, by playing offbeats and fast interlocking patterns.

You can see and hear how this works in practice by visiting the 'gamelan mecanique' website (www.citedelamusique.fr/gamelan/shock.html). Listen to the first piece played on the Central Javanese gamelan: *Lancaran*. One cycle of the core instruments has been transcribed below:

Heterophony

Gamelan music is often described as having a **heterophonic** texture: most instruments play the same basic melody but elaborate it in different ways.

For example, you can see in the music above that the peking – like the larger sarons – also plays the balungan but simply doubles up every note. The kempul, in contrast, simply misses out every other note (with an extra rest in the first bar).

In *Lancaran*, the bonang and kenong focus solely on the two most important notes in the balungan: the B and G♯. When every other instrument simply doubles up the notes of the balungan, you may wonder why the bonang and kenong play a B in bar 4 rather than a G♯, which would seem like a more logical choice. This is because of another important feature in gamelan music: **anticipation**. Instruments frequently anticipate the notes of the core melody; in *Lancaran*, the bonang and kenong both anticipate the first note of the balungan, playing it a bar before the saron does.

Gamelan often include other melody instruments such as rebab, suling or voice, and although these also generally elaborate on the core melody, they have much greater rhythmic freedom than the other gamelan instruments. As a result, they tend to add a floating layer over the clockwork-like texture created by the rest of the gamelan.

LISTENING EXAMPLE

Having become familiar with the piece *Lancaran*, listen again to the second Central Javanese piece on the 'gamelan mecanique' website: *Ladrang*. Ask your students the following questions (you may need to mute different instruments to work out the answers!):

1. The core melody of *Ladrang* is much longer than the balungan for *Lancaran*. How many notes does it have? (32)
2. How do you know when you've completed a whole cycle and returned to the first note of the balungan? (You hear the gong ageng)
3. How many different sounds are the kendhang making? (Three)
4. The kenong is one of the instruments that divides the gongan into smaller chunks. In *Ladrang*, does it divide the gongan into two halves or four quarters? (Four quarters)
5. Which quarter of the melody uses a descending sequence? (The last one)
6. How does the bonang barung relate to the balungan? (The bonang anticipates every other main melody note by a minim beat. It also decorates the melody by adding in extra notes that, again, anticipate the

notes of the balungan. This is easiest to see when notated; the first half of the melody is elaborated by the bonang as follows:

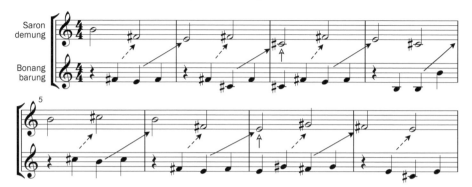

Here you can see that:

* Every balungan note that falls on the first beat of the bar is played a minim beat early by the bonang (as indicated by the solid black arrows).
* Each of these notes steps down from, and then returns to, a repeated note that again anticipates a balungan note by a crotchet beat (as indicated by the dashed arrows, although note the exception in bar 4).
* To create a bit of variation, every four bars (starting from bar 2), the bonang also doubles the balungan note on the first beat of the bar (as indicated by the white arrows).

This is a typical example of a gamelan pattern that seems complicated but actually derives from the balungan in a logical and straightforward way. Following the principles given above, can your students work out the bonang part for the second half of the melody?)

7. Describe two differences between the two bonang parts. (The bonang panerus essentially plays the same part but an octave higher, and twice as fast – so each three-note phrase is repeated twice)

PERFORMING

A transcription of *Ladrang* is provided on the book website. You could recreate this piece by using instruments such as the following:

* Kendhang: congas/bongos/djembes
* Bonang, saron and kenong: glockenspiels/xylophones/vibraphones/keyboards

* Ketuk: any percussion instrument that creates a short, 'dead' sound
* Gongs: cymbals or a very low note on the piano (played with the sustaining pedal).

The most 'authentic' way to teach this piece is without notation. A good place to start is by teaching everyone to play the core melody. You could then ask the peking, bonang and kenong players to work out their own parts given basic instructions (such as: the peking plays the balungan but repeats each note, so appears to play twice as fast as the saron demung).

Gamelan musicians usually learn to play all of the instruments in an ensemble, and frequently swap places in rehearsals or even performances. You could ask your students to do the same: can they swap instruments and teach each other how their new part should go?

As kendhang drummer, try speeding up and slowing down your ensemble by playing loud crotchet notes towards the end of a cycle, which either get faster or slower. Your students will have to listen carefully to maintain the right tempo, and this is a great way for them to practise their ensemble skills! Gamelan pieces often speed up just before the last cycle of a performance and then slow right down for the end; can your ensemble do this?

COMPOSING

The structure and principles of gamelan music are easy to replicate in a composition project. In groups, your students could write and perform their own gamelan pieces using instruments such as glockenspiels and keyboards. Alternatively, programs such as Logic, Cubase and Reason are excellent for composing repetitive music, and offer a good range of instrumental sounds.

The following steps will help your students to compose a piece of gamelan music:

1. Choose a pentatonic scale on which to base the piece (such as C, D, F, G, A).
2. Write a 16 or 32-note balungan (divided into 8-note phrases). Each note in this balungan should last for a minim. Balungan melodies tend to have a meandering quality, but one or two notes are likely to stick out more than the others. Frequent large leaps are uncommon.
3. Write a part for the kenong that doubles every second or fourth note of the balungan.

4. Write a part for the peking that repeats every note of the balungan (at a crotchet pace).
5. Write a part for the kempul, which should double or anticipate some of the balungan notes.
6. Write offbeat patterns for the bonang that add a faster layer to the music. These should also double or anticipate the notes of the balungan.
7. Don't forget to add in the gong ageng.
8. Write a simple drum pattern to accompany the gamelan.
9. Students could also add a melody line for suling or rebab, loosely based on the balungan but with added ornamentation and extra rhythmic freedom.

CROSS-CURRICULAR LINKS

Art/Drama/English link: the most obvious cross-curricular link when it comes to gamelan music is to create and stage your own shadow-puppet play. This could involve:

*   Writing a script, which could be adapted from one of the Hindu epics
*   Making the puppets (for example by using stiff card and paper fasteners to create moving parts)
*   Composing gamelan music to accompany any scenes of the play that feature action rather than talking
*   Rehearsing and performing the play (complete with gamelan accompaniment).

Religious Education link: gamelan also presents a good opportunity to introduce students to the fundamentals of Islam, Hinduism and Buddhism.

RESOURCES

The widespread popularity of gamelan outside of Indonesia means there is a great collection of resources available to help teach it, a few of which are targeted specifically at UK schools. The section below mentions some of the most useful resources for the music teacher.

Workshops

There are numerous organisations throughout the UK who can provide school workshops. Some of these will be able to bring a gamelan directly into your school, while others require you to visit the gamelan in situ. It may be that your local music education hub can provide workshops; otherwise, search for local providers online or investigate concert venues such as the Southbank Centre or Royal College of Music (which both host gamelan workshops as part of their education programmes).

A list of UK gamelan locations is provided on this website, and may be a useful place to start: www.gamelan.org.uk/uklist.htm.

Websites

* Gamelan mecanique (an interactive online gamelan): www.citedelamusique.fr/gamelan/shock.html
* Wells Music Academy 'virtual gamelan' (a free downloadable program designed especially for schools): http://www.academy. wellscathedralschool.org/free-resources
* Southbank Centre gamelan (this website lists performances and workshops, but also has a useful background section called 'About gamelan'): www.southbankcentre.co.uk/gamelan/.

Books

* *A Gamelan Manual: a player's guide to the Central Javanese gamelan* by Richard Pickvance (Jaman Mas Books, 2005): a practical guide to Central Javanese gamelan that is generally considered to be a must-have if you are learning this style of music.
* *Focus: gamelan music of Indonesia* by Henry Spiller (Routledge, 2008): a fairly academic book that provides a comprehensive overview of Indonesian gamelan.
* *Teach & Play Balinese Gamelan* by Mike Simpson (Rhinegold Education, 2012): a book of six Balinese gamelan pieces designed for school use, accompanied by a DVD.

SAMBA

WHY TEACH SAMBA?

Most associated with the southern Brazilian cities of Rio de Janeiro and São Paulo, samba combines African rhythmic roots with Latin exuberance and passion. Any students who like music that is loud, extrovert and rhythmic will be drawn to samba, and any who like to party will love Rio's Carnival celebrations: this is surely a world music for the world's youth.

By studying samba you can:

* Introduce students to the vibrant culture of a country that is on its way to becoming a major global power, having one of the world's fastest growing economies.
* Include all students in the rhythmic drive of the music: it's a great style for classroom participation.
* Encourage students to engage with extra-curricular music-making: samba bands are 'cool' and will get noticed!

A BRIEF HISTORY

Origins

There are 13 countries on the continent of South America. Brazil is the largest of these (it is world's fifth largest nation). Although it borders all but two of the other South American countries, it is set apart from all of them in some significant ways. Brazil is, above all, the land of the Amazon and its rainforest. It is also the only Portuguese-speaking country on the continent, having been a colony of Portugal from 1500 until independence in 1822.

Above all, however, it is the South American country closest to Africa. It is believed that around 35% of all Africans who were shipped to the Americas during the **slave trade**, between the 16th and 19th centuries, were taken to Brazil: in all around 3 million people. They were shipped to Brazil to work in the mines and, in particular, on the sugar-cane plantations.

This African dimension is at the heart of samba. The slaves were shipped across the Atlantic more or less empty-handed, but this couldn't stop their music and culture from finding new ways to take root in Brazilian soil. Soon the eastern regions of Brazil, notably Bahia, were being strongly influenced by African cultural practices, such as the Candomblé religion and the rhythms of African music.

Today samba is found throughout Brazil, even in Manaus, deep in the Amazon rainforest. It is most associated, however, with the southeastern coastal city of **Rio de Janeiro**.

Samba emerges in Rio

Slavery in Brazil was finally abolished in 1888. At least 200,000 black slaves in Rio became liberated. By the turn of the 20th century, many slaves from other parts of the country were also migrating to Rio in search of a new livelihood. The influx led to the building of shanty towns on the hillsides of the city. Initially called *bairros Africanos*, these areas in time became known as *favelas*. It is in the favelas of Rio that samba took root.

It is not easy to define exactly what samba was at this stage. For some it was a dance that was performed by a couple touching navel-to-navel, for others a type of song. *Rodas de samba* (samba sessions) would be held in the back yards and houses of the *tias baianas* – the female descendents of black slaves from the Bahia region. These gatherings were often disrupted by the police.

A few early recordings were made of songs under a 'samba' label, although they didn't achieve popularity. Then in 1917 a musician with the nickname '**Donga**' (real name Ernesto dos Santos) released a recording of his song *Pelo telephone* ('By telephone'), which is now considered to be the first true samba song.

You can listen to *Pelo telefone* in YouTube video 'Samba 1: Telefone'. As a rather charming ballad, this historic recording may sound a long way from your expectation of what samba is, but listen carefully: throughout, the accompanying cavaquinho (a small guitar) has the rhythm ♪♫ on alternate beats. This is one of the hallmark rhythmic patterns of samba today.

1920–1950: samba blossoms

Initially viewed with suspicion (not least because of its black roots) by the middle classes, who were formed largely of European immigrants, the rhythms and melodies of samba were soon taken up by people of all backgrounds in the city. Various subgenres of the style emerged, including:

* **Samba-canção**: a slower style in which the lyrics often focus on sadness, love, disillusion and betrayal. One example is *Ninguem me ama* ('Nobody loves me'), a 1954 hit sung by Nora Ney. See YouTube video 'Samba 2: Ney'.
* **Samba de partido alto**: often simply called 'partido', songs of this category are characterised by a prominent beat on the pandeiro (see page 128) and have a verse-refrain structure that allows for everyone to participate in the refrain. Verses are sometimes sung by different solo singers, adding an element of competition. A popular example is *Perdoa* by Paulinho da Viola – see YouTube video 'Samba 3: Viola'.

Samba also began to spread internationally. One of the significant musicians in this regard was the Brazilian singer **Carmen Miranda**, who in the 1940s and 50s was a Hollywood film star. She appeared in over 20 films, many with Latin American themes (such as *That Night in Rio* in 1941 and *Copacabana* in 1947).

Leading samba musicians from the first half of the 20th century		
Ary Barroso	Angenor de Oliveira (known as 'Cartola')	Noel Rosa
1903–1964	1908–1980	1910–1937
Pianist, composer and football commentator!	Singer and composer.	Guitarist, banjo player and composer.
One of Brazil's most successful songwriters of the 20th century.	Composed over 500 songs in a long career broken by a disappearance in the 1940s and 50s. Often wrote slower sambas.	Wrote over 250 songs, often with witty or ironic lyrics that made a social commentary. Died young from tuberculosis.
Listen to *Aquarela do Brasil* (YouTube video 'Samba 4: Barroso').	Listen to *O sol nascerá* (YouTube video 'Samba 5: Cartola').	Listen to *Com que roupa?* (YouTube video 'Samba 6: Rosa').

CARNIVAL

Today, the most famous manifestation of the samba tradition is Carnival. This festival occurs in the days leading up to Ash Wednesday and the season of Lent. Parades happen in many Brazilian cities and villages, but the most spectacular is in Rio de Janeiro.

The origins of the Rio Carnival date back to the 18th century, i.e. before the development of samba. Back then European dances – waltzes, polkas, mazurkas, and so on – would be performed. Now samba rules and it is a euphoric expression of Brazilian identity.

Carnival in Rio

The Rio Carnival has been called 'the greatest show on earth', and it is hard to disagree:

* The Carnival season starts in January – a hot summer month in Rio.
* More than 300 street bands provide outdoor parties across the city, attracting up to 500,000 foreign visitors.
* The culmination is four days of parades at the specially designed open-air Sambadrome – a 700m route with tiered stands either side for 90,000 spectators – at which samba schools (see below) compete and are assessed by a jury.
* Parades in the Sambadrome start at about 9pm and continue until the morning.
* Flamboyant, colourful costumes dominate the spectacle, which is accompanied by the exuberant and thunderous beat of the samba bands.
* Results are published on Ash Wednesday, with a winners' parade the following Saturday.

During Carnival the normal boundaries of society in Rio are removed. Rich and poor can both share in the celebrations. Indeed, traditionally aristocrats would dress as commoners while the poor would dress as princes and princesses.

YouTube video 'Samba 7: Carnival' is a short documentary that gives a suitably colourful introduction to the Carnival celebrations (note that this video, along with almost all footage of the Rio Carnival, includes a number of women in very skimpy costumes!).

Samba schools

The main parades in the Carnival are a competition between a series of organisations called samba schools (*escolas de samba*). These are more than just establishments that teach and perform samba: each one is the focal point for a neighbourhood, servicing a variety of community needs including education and medical care. Samba schools are largely run by volunteers, and it is rumoured that the drug lords contribute funds to the schools – a kind of guardianship of their shanty-town community.

The first samba school to be called as such, Deixa Falar ('Let them talk'), was founded in 1928, parading for the first time the following year. The idea quickly caught on: in 1930 there were five schools parading in the Carnival, and a competition between them was declared. Deixa Falar won, repeating the victory in 1931. By 1932, 19 sambas schools were represented. Today there are over 70, each with their own colours, and an entire league system of six divisions with promotion and relegation. Citizens of Rio support a samba school as we might a football team (mind you, football is also enormous in Brazil...).

The 'Premiership' is called the Special Group (*grupo especial*) and then there are groups A, B, C, D and E. The top three groups parade in the Sambadrome; the others on the streets of the city. There are 14 schools in the Special Group; each year the lowest-rated parade causes that school to be demoted to Group A, and the top-scoring school from the 10 schools in Group A is promoted for the following year.

Two of the most significant schools are:

* **Mangueira**: founded in 1929 by the musician Cartola, among others. Mangueira has green and pink as its colours; the school has won 18 carnival titles, the most recent in 2002. See YouTube video 'Samba 8: Mangueira'.
* **Portela**: founded in 1935, Portela has the colours blue and white. The school has won more championships than any other (21) including seven in a row in the 1940s. See YouTube video 'Samba 9: Portela'.

The samba parade

Each samba school's parade is an enormous production. Special Group parades feature 3,500–5,000 people, and even the lowest-division schools that parade at the Sambadrome (Group B) will have around 1,500 people performing. Each school has a maximum of 1 hour 30 minutes to parade the 700m of the Sambadrome. Traditionally, there are various common elements that make up the presentation prepared by each school. Some of these are:

* The **comissão de frente** (vanguard group): a compulsory first element made up of around 10–15 people who introduce the school's theme for the year. Originally this consisted of well-dressed men; nowadays it is a more extrovert spectacle including the first float of the parade.
* The **mestre-sala** (master of the room) and **porta-bandeira** (flag bearer): the flag bearer carries the school's flag, while the master of the room dances around her according to detailed rules (for example they must never dance back-to-back).
* The **baianas**: at least 80 older women dressed in glitzy versions of the traditional dress from the Bahia region, paying tribute to the African immigrant roots of samba.
* The **bateria** (drum section): the beating heart of the parade with up to 350 percussionists, mainly drummers. Often there is a female dancer at the front of the bateria who is supposed to inspire the male drummers.
* The **singers**: usually a well-known lead male singer with a backing group who sing the school's specially composed samba song for the parade.
* The **carro alegorico**: the procession of floats that depict the school's chosen theme.

The judging panel assesses each samba school on 10 categories:

1. The vanguard group
2. The flag-bearer
3. The bateria
4. The samba song
5. 'Harmony' – the blend of music and choreography
6. Flow and spirit
7. The theme of the year
8. Floats and props
9. Costumes
10. Overall impression.

Themes range from the historical and mythological to political and environmental. Some themes of the last few decades include:

Theme	Samba school	Year
Capitães do asfalto ('Captains of the road', referring to the children who live on the streets of Rio)	Sao Clemente	1987
Trevas! Luz! A Explosão do Universo ('Darkness! Light! Explosion of the universe')	Viradouro	1997
Villa-Lobos e a Apoteose Brasileira (A tribute to the famous Brazilian composer Heitor Villa-Lobos)	Mocidade	1999
Um Mundo sem Fronteiras ('A world without frontiers')	Rocinha	2005
A Lendas das Sereias e os Mistérios do Mar ('The legend of the mermaids and the mysteries of the sea')	Império Serrano	2009

INSTRUMENTATION

Depending on the style, samba can use a wide range of pitched and un-pitched instruments. Parades tend to favour the louder brass and percussion instruments; samba-canção songs might indulge in the softer timbres of strings or flute. The guitar is a common presence, as is the distinctive cavaquinho.

Cavaquinho: this is a small guitar of Portuguese origin. The most common tuning is D–G–B–D, although guitarists sometimes tune the upper string to E so that the instrument matches the top four strings of the guitar. The cavaquinho enables the harmony of samba to be projected with a strumming, percussive edge (the high pitch, when coupled with wire strings, gives the instrument greater projection than the guitar). Various clips can be found on YouTube; video 'Samba 10: cavaquinho' shows both the harmonic and melodic possibilities of the instrument.

The bateria

The instruments of the bateria (drum section) help to create the distinctive sound of Carnival-style samba.

Surdo: this is the foundation of the bateria: a large bass drum that is worn from a shoulder or waist strap so that the skin faces upwards. The shell of a surdo can be made from wood, steel or aluminium; the head from goatskin or plastic.

The drum is played with a single beater (with the other hand used to stop the sound). Three distinct teams of surdo players are found in the standard bateria:

1. **Surdo primeira** or **maracaçáo:** the 'marker' of the pulse. These players use the largest drums (22–26in), and establish the pulse by playing on the second beat with the beater, stopping the sound on the first beat with the left hand:

2. **Surdo segunda** or **resposta:** the 'response' to the primeira. These players use slightly smaller drums (20–22in) and play on the first beat with the beater, stopping the sound on the second beat with the left hand:

3. **Surdo terceira** or **cortador:** the drum that cuts across the pulse of the other surdos. These players use the smallest surdo drums (16–18in), and play more complex patterns that provide syncopations and impetus to the basic pulse. Terceira players are the only surdo players who are permitted to improvise.

Some samba schools are known for particular terceira patterns. For example, the following pattern is associated with the Mocidade samba school.

See for example YouTube video 'Samba 11: surdo terceira'.

Caixa: this is the Portuguese name for the **snare drum**, which in samba parades is usually worn on a shoulder strap. The caixa typically plays semiquavers, with some patterns using accents to bring out syncopated Latin rhythms. Two basic patterns are:

See for example YouTube video 'Samba 12: caixa'.

Chocalho and reco-reco: the chocalho is a type of **shaker**, with a number of jingles set in a frame. This is rhythmically shaken, usually in semiquavers. Chocalho players are customarily placed at the front of the bateria. See for example YouTube video 'Samba 13: chocalho'.

A similar role is played by the reco-reco: a type of **scraper** like a guiro.

Agogo: this consists of two **cowbells** joined by a U-shaped piece of metal. Its origins go back to the immigrants' roots in Africa. The bells are struck with a wooden stick; it is also possible to squeeze them together to create a click sound. Two common patterns are:

See for example YouTube video 'Samba 14: agogo'.

Tamborim and pandeiro: the name 'tamborim' reminds us of 'tambourine', but it's not quite the same: this is a very **small drum** with a taut plastic head. It is held in one hand while being hit with a flexible plastic stick in the other. The shallow depth of the frame allows the sound to be adjusted by pressing your fingers on the underside of the skin. The tricky playing technique known as *virado* – where the drum is flipped over in the middle of a pattern – also creates variations in the sound. The tamborim usually plays semiquavers that make use of the virado technique; see for example YouTube video 'Samba 15: tamborim'.

The pandeiro, however, is essentially a **tambourine**. It differs from a standard classroom tambourine in that the head can be tightened by screw threads around the rim of the drum. In addition, the jingles are cupped to give a crisper tone and greater clarity when played at a fast tempo.

Given the speed at which the pandeiro is played (usually semiquavers) and the playing technique (which variously involves using the thumb, fingers, heel and palm of the hand), the pandeiro is full of subtlety and flair, and not at all simple to master. See for example YouTube video 'Samba 16: pandeiro'.

Cuica: this is an unusual drum with a very distinctive squeaky sound. It is a small drum with a single head, with a stick attached to the skin inside the drum. The player pulls a damp cloth along the stick to create a sound; the pitch of this can be altered by pressing down on the drum head with the thumb of the non-playing hand. See for example YouTube video 'Samba 17: cuica'.

Repinique: one further drum in the bateria that plays a very significant role. Often the musical director of the bateria is one of the repinique players. The drum is similar to the **tom-tom**: it is double-headed and has a 12in metal shell with a nylon head. In Rio it is worn from a shoulder strap and played with a stick in one hand (the other hand is also used to slap the head of the drum). A typical repinique pattern is:

See for example YouTube video 'Samba 17: repinique'.

Apito: this is a small referee-like **whistle** that can play up to three different notes. It is essentially used to 'conduct' the bateria; the leader of the bateria will frequently play a phrase on the apito, accompanied by a particular hand symbol, to signal a change in the music (such as when to begin a new section or rhythm).

CHARACTERISTIC FEATURES OF THE STYLE

Samba is one of those styles that you know instantly when you hear it. The characteristic elements of a Carnival-style samba piece include:

* A busy percussive accompaniment that features the bateria instruments
* A strummed harmonic accompaniment provided by the cavaquinho
* A $\frac{2}{4}$ metre and brisk tempo
* Syncopation and the use of complex rhythms
* A song that features a repeated refrain or section that is sung in unison by a chorus of backing singers
* A major key and reliance upon the primary chords.

Beginning a piece

Beyond this, listen out for the way that the bateria signal the start and end of a song. There are certain formulae that are used to set a samba piece underway, in a way not unlike the drummers of a military marching band. The repinique is often the instrument that introduces a samba piece. For example:

Finishing a piece

Likewise, there are particular phrases that conclude a samba piece (which are signalled by the apito). For example:

LISTENING EXAMPLE

For an example of a typical samba piece of the kind you would hear in the Rio Carnival, listen to 'Brasiliana' from the album *Carnival in Rio* (available on Spotify and iTunes). In particular, listen out for:

* The bateria with its rich range of unpitched timbres
* Flamboyant strumming on the high-pitched cavaquinho
* Occasional interruptions from the apito whistle
* Singing that alternates between a solo male voice and a large chorus (in unison).

In addition, listen out for these two melodic phrases that occur more than once:

Phrase A:

Phrase B:

An outline to the structure of the song is as follows:

0:00	The track starts with the bateria: listen out for the strong surdo part (playing on beats 2 and 4), and the high-pitched cuica.
0:14	The bateria stop their repetitive patterns momentarily to allow the cavaquinho – which starts playing at this point – to be heard.
0:22	The bateria resume their patterns and the chorus sings phrase A twice.
0:36	The soloist sings the first verse.
0:56	The chorus sing phrase B (which is a repeat of the soloist's last line).
1:03	The soloist sings the second verse.
1:37	The chorus sing phrase B (again a repeat of the soloist's last line).
1:44	The soloist sings the third verse.
2:20	A lengthy section for the chorus begins, which includes phrase A (at 2:27) and phrase B (at 2:54).
3:07	The surdo pattern becomes a little more elaborate, having previously just marked the beat.
3:49	The soloist sings the fourth verse.
4:17	A brief drum fill introduces the final section, with soloist and chorus in unison (listen out for the cuica and apito as well).

PERFORMING

A simple arrangement of the famous first ever samba song, *Pelo telefone*, is provided on the book website. There are various ways in which you might involve your students in performing this song:

* Some can sing
* Guitarists can strum the chords given – use the rhythm of the right-hand piano part
* Bass guitarists can play the left-hand piano part
* Others can use some of the rhythm patterns mentioned earlier in the chapter to construct appropriate bateria-style percussion parts.

Should you wish to sing along to the original recording (YouTube video 'Samba 1: Telefone'), you will have to perform the song in D♭ major – a transposed copy for doing this can also be found on the book website.

COMPOSING

This project will allow your students to write their own samba song, by choosing appropriate musical jigsaw pieces to set the following lyrics in a suitably Brazilian style.

This is no sombre samba to idly sidle a slight sashay,
This is no rumbling rumba to humbly bumble the night away,
This is a drivin' groovin' beat that enters your jivin' movin' feet, so:
Come on, let's scramble, mama skedaddle! Go dance the samba way!

Step one: choosing the rhythm for the melody

Before your students can write a melody for the singer, they need to work out a rhythm for the lyrics. They should:

1. Remember that samba is usually in a $\frac{2}{4}$ metre with a brisk pulse.
2. Imagine trying to sing (or rap) the lyrics to a pulse, and highlight the syllables that naturally need emphasis. For example: ***This*** *is no* **som**-*bre* **sam**-*ba...*
3. Use the following jigsaw pieces to create a rhythm for the lyrics. Each highlighted syllable should be attached to the **first** note on a jigsaw piece.

4. Each jigsaw piece counts as one beat (half a bar). Your students can use each piece as many times as they want to put together a rhythm for the whole verse.

Step two: choosing a chord progression

If your students look at the music for *Pelo telefone* (available to download from the book website), they will see the chord symbols above the piano staves. Notice the following points:

* With the exception of the introduction/interlude, chords do not change often
* Chords normally change at the beginning of the bar
* By far the most commonly used chords are C and G^7 – the tonic (I) and dominant 7th (V^7).

Your students should now choose a pattern of chords (each probably lasting for a complete bar – or even several bars) from the jigsaw pieces below. This can be successfully done by just using the first two jigsaw pieces (C and G^7), but your students may like to use some of the others as well, especially for the third line of the lyrics.

Step three: choosing the notes for the melody

By now your students should have the rhythm of their melody and a chord for each bar. It is time to use these to create a memorable tune that is catchy and easy to sing.

Students should use notes from the chords for the basis of their melody, so that the tune fits the harmony. Other notes can be used with care, especially if they are approached by step.

Step four: finishing touches

By now your students will have the essential parts of a samba song in place: the rhythm, the harmony, the melody and the phrase structure. In order to turn this into a polished piece they may like to think about the following:

* Which instruments should play the chord progression?
* What rhythms should these instruments play?
* What instruments should be in the bateria?
* What patterns should these percussionists play?
* How should the piece start and finish?

If your students want to extend their compositions further, they might like to write a second verse of lyrics. The words for this verse need to fit the tune they have already composed. They might also like to construct a chorus or refrain section, to link the two verses together.

An example composition that follows the steps above is provided on the book website.

CROSS-CURRICULAR LINKS

Business/Economics link: Brazil is one of the 'BRIC' countries – an acronym used to group together four countries that have similar, rapidly developing economies (the other three being Russia, India and China). The 'BRIC' countries have come to represent a shift in global economic power from developed to developing countries, and as such can make an interesting cross-curricular topic to study.

Art/Dance link: the floats, costumes and dances in the Rio Carnival are just as integral to a samba school's parade as the music. Could your school host its own mini-Carnival? This could bring together various elements from different departments: the bateria and official samba song from the Music department; the dancers (including a flag bearer and master of the room) from the PE/Dance department; the costumes, masks, official samba-school flag and even floats from the Art department.

RESOURCES

There are numerous organisations and samba schools in the UK who can provide school workshops. If an online search doesn't bring up local providers, the website of the UK and Irish Samba Association may help (www.uksamba. org): it includes a map of samba bands in the UK.

The following books are most relevant for the music teacher:

* *Teach & Play Samba* by Mike Simpson (Rhinegold Education, 2012): a book of six samba pieces designed for school use, accompanied by a DVD.
* *Rhythm Matters: Introduction to Samba Batucada* by Ravin Jayasuriya (One Voice Music, 2010): an ebook that teaches you how to play basic samba rhythms on various bateria instruments, leading to the performance of a complete piece.
* *The Beatlife Book: Playing & Teaching Samba* by Chris Preston and Stuart Hardcastle (Soar Valley Music, 2008): a book that teaches you various samba rhythms and includes advice on pedagogy, accompanied by a CD.
* *The Brazilian Sound: Samba, Bossa Nova and the Popular Music of Brazil* by Chris McGowan and Ricardo Pessanha (Temple University Press, 1998): a book that provides a good overview of a variety of Brazilian genres.

TANGO

WHY TEACH TANGO?

Possibly the most sensuous of all the world's dances, it is not just the dancers who convey the passion and heartache of tango: the music exquisitely and viscerally captures both emotions.

Away from the Europeanised tango of the ballroom (and *Strictly Come Dancing*), the home of tango is deep in the south of South America – most notably in the bohemian quarters of Buenos Aires, capital of Argentina.

The sound of Argentine tango, with its bittersweet bandoneon timbre, is likely to capture your students' imagination as much as the passionate moves of the dancers.

There are several dimensions that can make tango a strong project in the classroom:

* A history of stylistic evolution
* Imaginative use of instrumentation
* A strong musical character created through specific features
* Ensemble performing that offers a range of technical challenges
* Exciting dancing opportunities.

A BRIEF HISTORY

Early days

The origins of tango date back to the **late 19th century**. It is generally believed to have begun in the **lower immigrant classes** of Buenos Aires. By the 1890s the majority of the population was immigrant, mostly men who worked in and around the docks. Here, at the brothels, musicians would play in popular styles while men waited for a girl, and music provided an opportunity to dance: thus tango evolved, initially with the men dancing together (the few girls were otherwise occupied).

In these early days, the music would have been played on whatever instruments were to hand, perhaps a flute and guitar. The immigrant communities brought their own musical skills. There was no bigger immigrant community in Buenos

Aires than the Italians, and they brought two particular musical enthusiasms – the voice and the violin.

Arrival of the bandoneon

Gradually tango moved up the social ladder (one can speculate that upper-class visitors to the brothels spread the word), aided by sales of gramophone records and sheet music for domestic use. A decisive step, however, was the arrival in Argentina of the **German bandoneon** in **1910**.

It is one of the strange quirks of musical history that the iconic sound of Argentine tango should be an instrument of German design. The bandoneon is a type of concertina developed in the 1840s and intended for itinerant church musicians to accompany hymn singing. The bandoneon makes a unique timbre: it completely suits the passionate quality of tango – music and dance – bringing out the heartache character.

Carlos Gardel, tango idol

The influence of immigrant Neapolitan song on the Argentine tango was very significant. Tango took a leap forward when, in 1917, a popular folk singer, Carlos Gardel, recorded *Mi noche triste* ('My sad night'). Although this was probably intended as a comic song, Gardel gave it a tragic, broken-hearted mood. This marked the start of a new direction of romantic, nostalgic songs, and through the 1920s the *tango-canción* (tango song) flourished. Gardel rose to stardom, idolised even more after his death in a plane crash at the age of 47.

Gardel recorded over 900 songs. In particular, look out for:

* *Mi noche triste*
* *Mi Buenos Aires querido*
* *Por una cabeza*
* *Volver*
* *Cuesta abajo.*

Various recordings of Gardel's work are available, often digitally re-mastered. The album *Carlos Gardel: 'El Zorzal Criollo'* is recommended. He also made the occasional film appearance (see for example YouTube video 'Tango 1: Gardel').

The golden age of tango

During the 1920s the tango band evolved into a fairly standard **sextet** of two bandoneons, two violins, double bass and piano. At the same time, the idolisation of the tango singer made the music less suitable for dancing. However this changed in the mid-1930s when, following the lead of Juan d'Arienzo's band, musicians brought greater rhythmic verve and energy to the playing style. This, perhaps coupled with Gardel's demise, reinvigorated the dance tradition of tango and gave birth to what is considered to be the golden age of tango.

Leading tango musicians from the golden age of tango

Aníbal Troilo	Horacio Salgán	Francisco Canaro
1914–1975	b. 1916	1888–1964
Bandoneonist and bandleader	Pianist and bandleader	Violinist and bandleader
Listen to *Palomita blanca* (YouTube video 'Tango 2: Troilo')	Listen to *A fuego lento* (YouTube video 'Tango 3: Salgán')	Listen to *Se dice de mi* (YouTube video 'Tango 4: Canaro')

After a **military coup** in 1955, Argentina entered a very bleak period of history that was to end in the Falklands War (or Malvinas War as it is called by Argentines) of 1982. The laws of the new regime banned young people from nightclubs where they might learn to tango, although turned a blind eye to them going to clubs playing rock and roll. With little demand for dancing tango, tango bands disappeared from the city scene.

Astor Piazzolla, master bandoneonist

Through the dark era of Argentine politics one Argentine musician flourished: Astor Piazzolla. He was born in Argentina in 1921, though most of his childhood was in New York, where he became familiar with the sounds of American jazz. Returning to Buenos Aires in 1937, he was soon playing bandoneon for Aníbal Troilo's tango orchestra.

Piazzolla's ambition to be a composer led him to study classical music with Alberto Ginastera, the greatest Argentine composer of the day, and then in Paris with Nadia Boulanger. She steered Piazzolla away from classical music and told him to write tango. So he returned to his native land and wrote tango, but not a conventional, pastiche tango: instead a raw, edgy *tango nuevo* ('new tango') rich in rhythmic energy, jazzy harmony and strange instrumental effects such as glissandos, tapping on the bandoneon and double bass, and gutsy 'shronking' noises made by the bow grating on the violin string.

Piazzolla's originality and the innovations he brought to tango made him unpopular among the traditionalists; Argentines have a saying that 'in Argentina everything may change, except the tango'. His great achievement was to reinvigorate tango and produce a style of instrumental tango music for listening to, rather than dancing to. Now his music is cherished in Buenos Aires and the top bands will all play some of his numbers.

There are many recordings of Piazzolla's music. Try to listen to those that are of his own performances: some of these are available to download for free at www.piazzolla.org/sounds/index.html. The following tracks are of particular appeal:

* *Libertango* (see YouTube video 'Tango 5: Libertango 1', with Yo Yo Ma on the cello. 'Tango 6: Libertango 2' features a couple dancing to this piece)
* *Adiós Nonino* (see 'Tango 7: Nonino', with Piazzolla on the bandoneon – this version omits a famous piano cadenza that is often played at the start of the piece)
* *Milonga del Angel* (see 'Tango 8: Milonga', also performed by Piazzolla)
* *Five Tango Sensations* (see 'Tango 9: Fear', a video of the fifth movement in the suite).

The modern era

Following the end of the Falklands War, Argentina returned to democracy in 1983 and with these happier times came a **renaissance** in tango. Young Argentines embraced tango anew, some reliving the old dancing tradition as taught by their grandparents, others taking the music in new directions such as found in the album *Tango Chill Sessions*. This rebirth also encouraged a new wave of tango exportation. For example, the hugely successful Gotan Project – a group that incorporates electronic elements into tango – formed in Paris in 1999. Finland, in particular, is one European country that has shown a great interest in tango.

The dance

Wonderful and intoxicating though the music of tango is, a major part of the tradition's appeal is its dance style: fiery and extrovert at times, sultry and intimate at others. If you are tempted to embark on a tango project, you may well want to collaborate with any colleagues who are expert in dance and can bring specialist knowledge to what you cover. So that you can identify some of the moves in the video clips you might be showing students, here are some of the more important terms:

* Abrazo – the embrace: unlike ballroom tango, the dancers hold each other close
* *Caminata* – the basic walk of tango
* *Ocho* – meaning eight: a common figure-of-eight step
* *Sacada* – a step in which the leader appears to knock the partner's leg away
* *Boleos* – a turning step that is interrupted, resulting in the follower's foot elegantly sliding on the floor at a slow tempo or flying into the air at a quick tempo
* *Gancho* – where one dancer's leg hooks around the leg of their partner.

INSTRUMENTATION

Argentine tango customarily uses a limited range of instruments: the iconic **bandoneon**, along with **violin, double bass, guitar** and **piano**. The standard tango quintet usually has one of each of these instruments; a sextet may have a second violin, or a second bandoneon. Some numbers of a group's repertoire may involve a singer.

Sometimes much larger groups – known in Spanish as an ***orquesta típica*** – are found, but it is rare to have other types of instruments involved. YouTube video 'Tango 10: Yumba', which is a performance of Pugliese's *La yumba,* shows the effect of massed ranks of bandoneons and violins. (Osvaldo Pugliese was a famous 20th-century tango pianist and arranger.)

The sound of the bandoneon, and the ways in which the other instruments are used, are at the centre of the tango sound.

The bandoneon

At the heart of the bandoneon is a pair of bellows. As the bellows are pulled out and pushed in, notes are produced by buttons on opposite ends of the instrument: 38

at the 'treble' end for the right hand, 33 at the 'bass' end for the left hand. Pushing in a button will cause the air to pass over a reed, in a similar way to a church harmonium – indeed, the bandoneon was intended to be a portable substitute for a church organ. Holding in a combination of buttons produces chords.

Many consider the bandoneon to be an instrument of torture. The arrangement of buttons seems rather arbitrary (not unlike the QWERTY keyboard first strikes someone who only knows the alphabet in order) and differs in the left hand to the right hand. It is also impossible to watch both hands simultaneously, so really the player needs to be able to memorise all fingering. The hardest thing of all is that each button plays two notes, one when the bellows are being opened, a different one when the bellows are being pushed together (and, lest you are wondering, it is not just a simple matter of transposition: the difference on some buttons may be just a semitone, on others much wider intervals!).

The sound of the bandoneon

For all its diabolical character, the bandoneon has a unique timbre: it suits the passionate quality of the tango perfectly, bringing out its heartache character. There are four particular effects to which the bandoneon is well-suited:

1. A long, expressive melody – single, long notes can swell as the air pressure is increased by the bellows. A good example is the start of Piazzolla's *Milonga del Angel* (YouTube video 'Tango 8: Milonga').

2. Agile, rapid quaver patterns – once fingering patterns are known each note is just one key, as on a piano, not a complex grouping of fingers. Watch Leopoldo Federico and his band playing *Al galope* in YouTube video 'Tango 11: Galope 1'. 'Tango 12: Galope 2' features a couple dancing to this piece.

3. Stabbing, staccato attacks – single notes and chords can be treated in this way as both bellows and buttons can contribute to the staccato effect. See for example the performance of Pugliese's *Malandraca* in 'Tango 13: Malandraca'.

4. Percussive tapping – created by tapping rhythms on the wooden sides of the bandoneon. A few examples can be heard and seen at the start of YouTube video 'Tango 14: Hora Cero', which is a performance of Piazzolla's *Buenos Aires hora cero*.

Use of the other instruments

After the bandoneon, the **violin** provides the main alternative melodic timbre in a tango ensemble. Tango composers enjoy both its rich low register (sometimes playing with a 'sul G' technique) and the sweet and soaring high register. Piazzolla's *Adios Nonino* demonstrates these contrasting tones: watch again YouTube video 'Tango 7: Nonino'. Also evident in this performance are some of Piazzolla's trademark use of advanced playing techniques, such as glissandos and scratching on the strings behind the bridge.

The **double bass** provides a strong bass line for the tango ensemble, though unlike in much jazz it is usually played with the bow. This can, however, be used with short, detached bowstrokes that dig into the string and give the bass line a strong rhythmic accentuation. The back of the instrument can also be tapped to add to the percussive element of the music.

The **piano** is also used to emphasise the bass line and increase the percussive nature of the music. In addition it provides the harmony of the music, and can be used for colouristic effects such as glissandos. Melodic lines sometimes appear in the piano part, and in later periods of tango these can be doubled at harsh intervals, such as 4ths and 7ths, to add a strong piquancy to the music.

Finally, the **guitar** – usually an electro-acoustic one – is used to provide a varied timbre for the harmony. It can also be used for countermelody lines, as at the start of Piazzolla's *Resurrección del angel* (YouTube video 'Tango 15: Angel').

CHARACTERISTIC FEATURES OF THE STYLE

Like jazz, tango comes in many varied manifestations. Yet once you have heard a little, you will instantly start to recognise the colours of the tango language. Tango can be slow or fast, instrumental or sung, in $\frac{4}{4}$ or a waltz. The most unifying element is the scoring – with the distinctive sound of the bandoneon to the fore.

Beyond that, there are some common features to look out for:

* A predominance of minor keys, but maybe moving to the tonic major for a middle section
* A strong, regular heavy beat
* Regular 8-bar phrases

* Diatonic chord progressions, often establishing the key with chords I and V⁷; brief visits to the relative major are characteristic
* Frequent changes of texture and scoring
* Tongue-in-cheek endings with a 'throw-away' soft cadence after a loud final section.

Like most dance styles, **rhythm** has a central role in tango music. There are some specific rhythmic patterns to look out for:

* A standard tango rhythm will have strong main beats and also an accented final quaver to each bar:

* A faster tango style called Milonga is in $\frac{2}{4}$ and mixes the following two rhythmic patterns, the first of which is derived from the habanera:

* Finally, the distinctive Latin accentuation of 3 + 3 + 2 will sometimes occur:

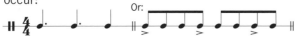

Most traditional tangos have clear sections with probably three (sometimes only two) ideas. A common structure is **ABCA**. It is standard practice for some sections to be repeated to bring contrasting timbres to the fore: so the violin might play the B section first, and the bandoneon will repeat it, maybe in an elaborated version.

LISTENING EXAMPLE

Most of these characteristic features can be found in *El choclo* by Angel Villoldo (1861–1919). This piece is an early classic from Argentine tango. The following timeline accompanies the recording by Quartango from the album *Performance*, highlighting the structure and some of the features of the scoring. (You can also watch Quartango perform this piece in the YouTube video 'Tango 16: Choclo', which is accompanied by dancing.)

Introduction	
0:00	Pizzicato bass with some rhythmic tapping on the side of the bandoneon. Note octave and rhythmic displacement in bars 3–4 (compared to bars 1–2 and 5–8).
0:11	Bandoneon enters with freely varied version of 'A' melody over bass groove. Note the interrupted cadence (V–VI) just before the introduction halts (0:33).
Section A	
0:38	Entry of piano and violin. Melody presented in D minor by bandoneon and violin, with heavy punctuating chords on beats 1 and 3.
0:43	More lyrically treated phrase, melody in violin with bandoneon an octave lower.
0:48	Phrase with strong offbeat chords (no chord on downbeat).
0:51	Final phrase of 'A' on bandoneon with violin countermelody below.
Section B	
0:55	Melody in piano, both hands – two octaves apart. Opening phrase suggests F major. Accompanying chords are in 3+3+2 rhythm.
1:04	Second half of 'B' melody in low violin register then higher bandoneon register. Returns to D minor.
1:12	Section B repeats. Same harmony, but melody is swapped for descending scales in 3rds – piano, violin, bandoneon. There is a simultaneous rising scale in the bass, at half speed with chromatic steps.
1:21	Second half of 'B' played lyrically on violin with bandoneon an octave lower.
Section C	
1:29	Music moves to D major. Melodic material carried by piano with 3+3+2 rhythm patterns. Listen out for short interjections by bandoneon (1:32) and violin (1:36).
1:37	Second half of 'C': melody in violin and bandoneon. Note the violin glissando (1:45) and imperfect cadence (1:43–1:45).
1:47	Section C repeats. Piano is an octave higher. Interjections now on bandoneon (1:49) and high-register double bass (1:53).
1:55	Second half of 'C': melody in violin and bandoneon. Perfect cadence at 2:01–2:03.
Section A	
2:03	Bandoneon gives short glimpse of opening theme (back in D minor). Violin then takes over with new expansive phrase (harmony as before). Bandoneon is used to inject chords on the offbeats (along with piano bass). A similarly scored answering phrase pattern starts at 2:16.
2:27	Music moves to G minor. Melody in upper violin register. Listen out for countermelody in lower register on bandoneon.

2:35	Listen for snippets of a countermelody in the piano middle octave, imitated a little lower on the bandoneon.
2:44	Bandoneon leads into slower final phrase which the violin again takes over, finishing in trills from 2:54.
Coda	
2:58	Coda starts with a mini-cadenza flourish on the piano.
3:04	There is a delightful cross rhythm created by the piano with 3+3+2 patterns. The bandoneon has pairs of notes outlining the main 'A' theme.
3:13	Violin takes over the melody as the music moves to C minor.
3:20	Bandoneon melody doubled by the violin a 6th lower.
3:24	Descending scales (reminiscent of 'B' section at 1:13) lead rapidly to a heavily weighted Neapolitan chord (D♭ major) at 3:26.
3:29	The main final perfect cadence: a prolonged chord V leading to chord I. Listen out for piano glissando at 3:31.
3:34	A trademark rapid V–I to give that unmistakable tango full stop.

PERFORMING

Few schools will know of a bandoneonist. Nonetheless, tango can be easily adapted for classroom performance, especially when you have one or more strong instrumentalists to play the melodic line.

El primero paso

El primero paso ('The first step') is an easy tango piece that combines a simple melody with the chord sequence to *El choclo*, and can be downloaded from the book website for your students to learn.

El choclo

An arrangement of *El choclo* is provided on the book website. The intention is that this arrangement can be adapted to fit a flexible range of scenarios and number of players. The essential elements are:

* The **melody** (top stave): this is a line for a good instrumentalist (or several) to learn. In keeping with tango tradition, you might like to have it played on a 'bandoneon' keyboard sound (possibly accordion) or give

it to a violinist, but it would also suit other instruments including flute or clarinet (an octave lower).

* The **harmony** (middle stave): the harmony of the piece is not complex. The chords required are given in the arrangement. These chords could be played in various ways: as pulsing quavers on guitars or keyboards, as sustained harmonies using string-pad sounds on keyboards, or with single notes of each chord (top/middle/bottom) played on separate instruments.

* The **bass** (lowest stave): a key part of the texture, the bass line needs to be strong. Ideally a double bass (with bow) would play this line. Bass guitar could be used. Imaginative alternative solutions might involve timpani.

* **Additional percussion** (not shown): further students could be asked to reinforce the tango rhythms, maybe just through clapping. Try experimenting with various options such as: first section – clap three quavers and then a semiquaver at the end of the bar; second section – clap the 3+3+2 pattern in each bar (thinking in semiquavers); third section – clap the following pattern:

The melody of *El primero paso* can also act as a countermelody to the start of *El choclo*.

An alternative way of performing the piece is as a piano duet. Some phrases could have the melody reinforced at the upper octave by the primo player.

COMPOSING

Tango can be a fertile style for gaining greater composing proficiency. On the one hand it is a style that can seem to have a very rigid, clichéd framework; engaging with this can deepen an inexperienced composer's understanding of harmony in particular. On the other hand it is a style that delights in nuance and wit; the search for this, and the experimentation the search involves, encourages a composer's imagination. In short, this is the classic combination of logical and creative thinking that all good composing demands.

This project is intended to address both halves of this synthesis. There is a fairly rigid chord sequence and a clear focus on structure. However, there are also plenty of suggestions for indulging in tango's potential for effect and surprise (these are highlighted as *stylistic extras*).

Two examples of the kind of piece one might produce with this project are available to download from the book website.

This project guides composers through the stages of writing a short instrumental tango for two melodic instruments and accompaniment, which is structured in clear sections.

Step one: instrumentation

Initially a decision needs to be made about instrumentation. Your students should have two melodic instruments and an accompaniment. They can choose one of the following packages:

1. The ideal **orquesta típica** option: lucky you – you know a bandoneonist! Write this piece for bandoneon, violin, piano and double bass.
2. The **alternative acoustic** option: no bandoneonist? Never mind: use a clarinet instead, along with violin as the melody instruments. The accompaniment can either be piano, or electro-acoustic guitar playing the chords and a bass guitar at the bottom.
3. The **computer-playback** option: let technology mimic the tango sound and select the instruments accordingly – look for a bandoneon and a violin for the melodies, and choose between piano and guitars for the accompaniment.

Step two: chord sequence for section A

Section A will comprise 16 bars of $\frac{2}{4}$ time. The key will be D minor to get that dark and sultry tango feel.

With the exception of bars 11–14, each chord will last for two bars, and will be emphasised on every beat by a crotchet chord of three notes – played either in the right hand of the piano, or on the guitar. Your students should follow this pattern of chords, choosing from the various suggestions at bar 12:

Bar 1	Bar 2	Bar 3	Bar 4	Bar 5	Bar 6	Bar 7	Bar 8
Dm	Dm	A^7	A^7	A^7	A^7	Dm	Dm

Bar 9	Bar 10	Bar 11	Bar 12	Bar 13	Bar 14	Bar 15	Bar 16
D^7	D^7	Gm	Dm Cm/E♭ E^7 B♭/A♭	Dm/A	A^7	Dm	Dm

Your students should think carefully about the order in which they write the notes for each chord, so that the line produced by the top notes does not leap around too much. For example, here is how the right-hand piano part might start:

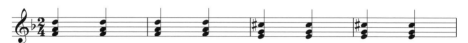

Step three: bass line for section A

The rhythm of the bass line (which will appear in either the piano left hand, double bass or bass guitar) should be:

The crotchet should usually be the root of the chord and the quaver the 5th, but your students can try experimenting with other options in the middle bars of section A, always choosing notes that are in the current chord.

Stylistic extra: students may like to occasionally use one of these alternative rhythms in the bass part, in which the triplet quavers or semiquavers need to be rising, conjunct shapes (possibly chromatic) leading up to the next crotchet:

You may like to give out the following version of the piano part to section A (also available to download from the book website), as a fast route to a guaranteed tango backdrop for students' work, and as a guide to working through section B and/or C later:

Step four: melody lines for section A

Your students should now have the harmonic backdrop for the first section of their tango and it is time to consider the melodic lines. The basic principles are:

* Think in 2- or 4-bar phrases
* Alternate which instrument has the tune
* Use fast, even notes early in the phrase (quavers or semiquavers)
* Let the fast notes lead to a longer note on a beat
* Start on a note that belongs to the chord underneath
* Use stepwise or arpeggio contours much of the time
* Finish the phrase with a leap.

Stylistic extra: some other good tips are:

* Start at least some phrases with a short (quaver or semiquaver) rest to inject momentum.
* Where there is a sharpened note in the chord, experiment with the natural version of the same note in the melody; similarly, where a 7th note occurs in a chord, it can be effective to use the sharpened version of this note in the melody.
* Let the two instruments overlap a little.
* A melodic note can be decorated by splitting it into triplets – the first and third of which are the same pitch as the original note, while the note in between is a step up or down.
* Let the note after a leap happen off the beat and make it accented (syncopated).

✱ Possibly use the occasional grace note (acciaccatura) to emphasise a note – these are most effective just a semitone below the main note (which might require the use of a sharp).

Putting all of this together, your students might start like this:

How many of the stylistic extras can your students see here?

Step five: sections B and C

Section B should be a complementary passage to section A that maintains the D minor focus, but starts with a brief turn towards the relative major. Here is the chord sequence – there are various options for bars 9–12, which are given below.

Bar 1	Bar 2	Bar 3	Bar 4	Bar 5	Bar 6	Bar 7	Bar 8
C⁷	C⁷	F	F	D⁷	D⁷	Gm	Gm

Bar 9	Bar 10	Bar 11	Bar 12	Bar 13	Bar 14	Bar 15	Bar 16
E♭⁷	E♭⁷	A♭	E⁷				
E⁷	E⁷	Am *or* F	B♭⁷	Dm/A	A⁷	Dm	Dm
G⁷	G⁷	Cm	E♭⁷				

Stylistic extra: it might be a good idea to give a 'kick' to the rhythm of the chords in this section, because by now everyone will be expecting the pulsating crotchet chords to keep going. A good way of doing this is to choose a pair of bars (starting with an odd-numbered bar) and use this rhythm pattern:

Your students should include the bass part if they do this, to break up its repetitive rhythm as well. For instance, bars 13–14 of section A above could be treated like this:

Or with an elaborated bass line:

Section C should be a more strongly contrasting section, for which the key changes to the tonic major (D major). Here is the chord sequence – once again there is an opportunity to select an option for bar 12:

Bar 1	Bar 2	Bar 3	Bar 4	Bar 5	Bar 6	Bar 7	Bar 8
D	D	A⁷	A⁷	A⁷	A⁷	D	D

Bar 9	Bar 10	Bar 11	Bar 12	Bar 13	Bar 14	Bar 15	Bar 16
F♯⁷	F♯⁷	Bm	Em E⁷ B♭⁷	D/A	A⁷	D	D

Stylistic extra: to enhance the sense of contrast, some change of texture is also advisable here. A good way of doing this is to have both melody instruments playing at the same time (rather than overlapping). This could be through doubling the melody at the octave, 6th or 3rd – and, remember, students could change which instrument is on top. A lighter texture in the piano, with more rests, might also help.

Step six: putting it all together

Depending on whether your students have worked through both sections B and C of this project, or just one or the other, below are various structures that can be used to create a complete piece.

In each case, section A occurs more than once, and your students should think about re-scoring this for each appearance (a strong aspect of the tango style). Remember that both the bandoneon and the violin can play chords, so between them they could look after the harmony for four or eight bars, giving the piano or guitar a chance to play the melody.

Here are some suggested structures:

* A A B B
* A A C A
* A B C A
* A A B C A
* A A B A C A.

Stylistic extra: each section ends with a D chord (D minor in sections A and B; D major in section C). This is a moment where a deft approach can capture something of the tango spirit. Here are some ideas that – give or take a change of F♮ for F♯ in section C – could work at the end of any section. Your students could either use one or more of these, or invent some endings of their own.

Other things to remember include dynamics, the use of staccato and accents, and various special effects such as pizzicato and glissandos in the violin part, instructions for the bandoneon to be tapped (not easy to replicate on computer playback), and so on.

Two complete example pieces are available to download from the book website.

CROSS-CURRICULAR LINKS

Spanish link: titles and lyrics for Argentine tango are always in Spanish – a potential gold mine for your Spanish-teaching colleagues, especially with recordings of tango-cancíons (songs) by the likes of Carlos Gardel and Roberto Goyeneche.

Art link: in the first half of the 20th century there was a thriving business in publishing tango hits of the day for domestic consumption. Sheet music was traditionally printed with eye-catching covers, often in an art-deco style. Searching online for 'tango sheet music covers' will bring up various examples; your students may like to study these and design their own to accompany their tango compositions.

History link: the history of Argentine tango is inextricably tied up with the social and political history of Argentina. You may like to explore the developing prosperity of the port of Buenos Aires in the early decades of World War II, the significance of the Perón government (which links with *Evita*), how tango went underground after the military coup of 1955, and its renaissance after the Falklands War of 1982.

RESOURCES

Argentine tango is today more popular internationally than ever before. There is a huge amount of material available, of which the following is inevitably but a small selection.

UK tuition and tango musicians

- ✱ Argentine tango in Scotland: www.scotlandtango.co.uk
- ✱ The Lincoln Tango Group: www.argentine-tango-lincoln.co.uk
- ✱ Tango UK (based near Southampton): www.tangouk.co.uk
- ✱ Tango Siempre, a leading UK tango band: www.tangomusic.co.uk

Books and sheet music

- ✱ *The Meaning of Tango* by Christine Denniston (Portico, 2007): a very useful, compact book on the Argentine tango tradition.
- ✱ A large amount of free tango music, in the form of versions for piano (that can provide the basis for your own arrangements) is available at www.mandragoratango.com/sheetmusic.php.
- ✱ Modern, professionally published tango music is available from various publishers. The catalogue of Tonos Music is outstanding: www.tonosmusic.com.

WEST AFRICAN MUSIC

WHY TEACH AFRICAN MUSIC?

The phrase 'African music', although useful for very broad generalisations, attempts the impossible in trying to sum up the music of an entire continent in two words. With over 50 countries and around 2,000 languages, Africa encompasses hundreds of musical styles and practices. It is celebrated globally for a number of musical genres, particularly its dance-drumming and vocal music.

Musically speaking, the continent is traditionally divided in two: north Africa and sub-Saharan Africa, with the Sahara desert providing a rough geographical dividing belt. North African countries such as Morocco, Algeria, Tunisia and Egypt all have their own musical traditions but share a broad influence of Arabic languages, musical systems and instruments. Below the Sahara, the Arabic influence recedes and hundreds of regional languages and musical styles create a diverse tapestry of musical practice. In this chapter we will focus on one part of the continent, west Africa, which is home to a number of styles (such as Ewe drumming, African blues and kora music) that are renowned throughout the world.

The study of African music has rightly become an accepted part of music education in the West. This is partly due to the relative ease with which students can learn simple drumming styles and successfully recreate them in the classroom. Such styles can be great for improving students' aural and ensemble skills, as well as their sense of rhythm. For Western students, African culture is generally vibrant, exciting and colourful to study. Due to its popularity in the West and in UK schools, African music is supported by a wide range of resources and workshop providers, making it one of the easiest world-music styles to study and teach.

A BRIEF HISTORY

The geographical region of 'west Africa' consists of 16 countries: Benin, Burkina Faso, Cape Verde, Côte d'Ivoire (Ivory Coast), The Gambia, Ghana, Guinea, Guinea-Bissau, Liberia, Mali, Mauritania, Niger, Nigeria, Senegal, Sierra Leone and Togo. The region has a very diverse climate, with lush tropical rainforest in the southern coastal region, a somewhat drier savannah to the north, and the semiarid 'Sahel' above this, which acts as a transition zone to the Sahara desert. The Niger River is the aqueous artery of much of the region, beginning in the highlands of Guinea and flowing for about 2,500 miles through Mali, Niger, Benin and Nigeria until it meets the Atlantic Ocean.

Pre-colonial history

The pre-colonial history of west Africa is dominated by the Ghana, Mali and Songhai Empires. Other smaller kingdoms and tribal groups have also featured in the region's complex history of territorial disputes. It is thought that the **Ghana Empire** began to develop around the 5th century under the Soninke people, and grew to dominate the west of the region until the 11th century. The empire lay about 500 miles to the north of present-day Ghana (in what is now Mauritania and Mali), and has no connection with the modern country other than providing a name for it when the new nation gained independence from Britain. The empire grew rich from gold and salt trading along the trans-Saharan trade routes, and also played an important role in establishing Islam in west Africa.

In the 12th century, the empire was absorbed and succeeded by the Mandinka people's **Mali Empire**. This expanded quickly in the 13th century by taking control of the gold and salt mines to the north and south, eventually becoming double the size of the Ghana Empire, covering much of modern day Guinea and Mali. It was a renowned centre of academic study and Islamic learning, particularly in the city of Timbuktu. After political infighting led to its demise and eventual collapse, the **Songhai Empire** became the dominant regional power in the 15th and 16th centuries. This empire was named after its people – the Songhai – and spread across Mali and Niger, becoming the largest and wealthiest empire in the history of west Africa.

Colonisation

The 15th century also saw the beginning of the European trade in gum arabic, gold and slaves. The Portuguese, Spanish, Dutch, French and British established trading posts along the west African coast. The **trans-Atlantic slave trade** really took off in the 16th century, and over the next few centuries it is estimated that around 12 million Africans were shipped from west and central Africa across to the Americas.

Between 1881 and the beginning of the First World War, the '**scramble for Africa**' saw European powers race to colonise the continent, and through a series of military campaigns they took control of the inland regions. In the end, France and Britain came out on top and colonised most of Africa (with France emerging as the dominant power in west Africa).

After the Second World War, partly spurred on by India gaining independence from the British Empire in 1947, the politician **Kwame Nkrumah** pushed for west African self-rule and was instrumental in the creation of an independent Ghana in 1957 (previously this country was a British colony named the Gold Coast). Other British and French colonies gained independence in the next few years; the last west African country to do so was the Portuguese colony of Guinea-Bissau in 1974.

In the decades following independence, the region has struggled with corruption, war and food shortages, but continues to strive for prosperity and political stability. Independence saw a surge in national pride in many west African countries, and cultural activities still remain important symbols of regional and national unity. Music and dance have both benefitted from this and feature high up the agenda in any display of regional or national cultural practice.

The wide range of musical genres in west Africa today encompasses both indigenous and colonial/Western influences, from traditional drumming ensembles dating back to pre-colonial times, to styles such as afropop that are heavily indebted to Western popular music. This chapter will later explore some of the main instruments and genres in west African music to give you a general overview of music in this region.

Music and religion

Religion in west Africa has been hugely influential in the development and practice of music. It broadly falls into three main types: local indigenous beliefs, Christianity and Islam. **Indigenous religions** predate the colonial era and exist in many forms throughout the region, with various local names. In general, local religions are monotheistic, with ancestral spirits (and those of the natural world) acting as intermediaries between man and God. Much of the traditional music of west Africa has its roots in this type of faith, with drumming, dance and song developing as an accompaniment to religious rituals and ceremonies.

During colonial times, much of this religion was suppressed and negative propaganda was spread as the locals were encouraged or forced to convert to **Christianity**. This is now the dominant religion in sub-Saharan Africa (including the southern coast of west Africa). Music plays a major role in Christian worship, and the singing of hymns (both of European and local origin) has given rise to a strong choral tradition in west Africa.

Islam dominates the rest of west Africa. As orthodox Islam doesn't use music for worship, Islamic contributions to the music of west Africa have been fairly minimal. (Arabic north African music, however, has had an influence, particularly in the upper regions of west Africa such as Mali, Mauritania and Niger.)

Griots

Griots (also known as 'jali') have a hugely important role in west African music. They are highly respected figures who essentially act as oral historians for a society, which they do by collecting, performing and passing down local stories, poems, genealogies, songs and instrumental music.

Griots have existed in west Africa for thousands of years, dating back to the Mali Empire. They are one example of a number of **endogamous castes** in west Africa (meaning that members of that caste are expected to marry within it); other examples of endogamous castes in this region include weavers, woodworkers and blacksmiths.

Griots tend to specialise in one of three areas: speech (such as storytelling and poetry), song or instrumental music. The **kora** is the instrument most strongly associated with the griot, although the balafon and ngoni are also instruments traditionally reserved for this caste. One of the most famous griot family names is **Diabaté** (also spelled Jobarteh), which dates back to the founding of the Mali Empire and has produced around 70 generations of griot musicians. Today the most famous of these is the Malian kora player Toumani Diabaté (his father Sidiki Diabaté recorded the first kora album in 1970, and his cousin Sona Jobarteh is the first female kora player to come from a griot family).

INSTRUMENTATION

West Africa boasts a wide variety of musical instruments. Some are specific to particular ethnic groups; others have originated with a particular group and spread to other parts of the region, taking on different designs and names as a result. The following section covers some of the most iconic west African instruments.

Drums and percussion

Djembe: this is probably the best-known African drum outside of the continent. It is thought to have originated among the Mandinka (or Malinke) people of the early Mali Empire. The drum has since spread to other west African countries such as Guinea, Ivory Coast, Burkina Faso and Ghana.

This goblet-shaped drum is carved from a single piece of hardwood such as *acajou* (cashew). The head, which is often made from goatskin, is attached to the top of the drum with an intricate rope lattice. The drum is played with the hands and has three main tones:

* The 'bass' sound, which is produced by slapping the hand in the centre of the head to create a rich, low sound.
* The 'tone' sound, produced by hitting the drum near the edge of the head to create a sharp, high sound.
* The 'slap' sound, produced by spreading the fingers apart and hitting the rim of the drum to create a piercing ring.

You can watch the master drummer Mamady Keita perform on the djembe in YouTube video 'African 1: djembe'.

Talking drum: many regional languages in west Africa are 'tonal', which means that changing the pitch of a word (or part of a word) can affect its meaning. There are various drums in west Africa that exploit this fact to mimic speech, although the precise ways in which they do so – and what they choose to convey – varies between different traditions. Some drums are traditionally used to communicate over long distances, calling a community together or transmitting news and warnings.

There are many west African drums that 'talk' to some extent, but there is one with a recognisable hourglass shape that is best known in the West as the 'talking drum'. In Africa it is given different names depending on the region; the Yoruba people in Nigeria, for example, call it the dundun.

This drum has a head at either end, attached to the drum by leather strings that run down the length of its body. It is struck with the fingers of the left hand and a curved wooden stick in the right hand. By holding the drum under one arm and squeezing the strings with the elbow (which tightens or loosens the head), a wide variety of pitches can be produced, allowing the drum to mimic the pitch inflections and rhythms of a particular language. A skilled drummer can even hold conversations and make jokes or social commentary with the instrument. YouTube video 'African 2: talking drum' demonstrates some of the capabilities of the instrument.

Dunun: originating among the Mande people of Guinea, this is another popular west African drum that also has the capacity to 'talk'. It is a cylindrical drum played with thick wooden sticks, and is often played in conjunction with a metal bell that rests on the top of the drum. It is commonly played in a group consisting of three different sizes: the large bass drum (dununba), the medium-sized treble drum (sangban) and the smallest soprano drum (kenkeni). YouTube video 'African 3: dunun' demonstrates all three sizes being played together.

Anlo-Ewe drumming ensemble: the Ewe people live in Ghana, Togo and Benin. The Anlo-Ewe are part of this group, living in the Volta region of southeast Ghana. They speak a local dialect of the Ewe language and are traditionally agriculturalists, fishermen and traders. They are also known for their polyrhythmic drumming, which is typically played by an ensemble consisting of the following instruments:

* **Astimevu**: the tallest drum in the ensemble, considered to be the father of the drum family. It is usually played by the master drummer, who uses it to lead the other drummers and to improvise solos.
* **Sogo**: a medium-sized drum described as the mother of the family. It produces a lower tone than the astimevu and usually plays supporting interlocking parts.
* **Kidi**: similar to the sogo but slightly smaller, and thought of as the older sister of the family. It sometimes enters into a dialogue with the master drummer.
* **Kaganu**: the smallest of all the drums, and the baby brother of the family. Unlike the other three drums, it isn't allowed to improvise but plays a fixed, repeated pattern throughout the whole piece.
* **Gankogui**: this instrument consists of two iron bells joined together at the handle. The two bells tend to be separated by an interval of a 4th or 5th. It plays a repeating ostinato that forms the foundation of the music, and acts as the timekeeper of the ensemble.
* **Axatse**: a gourd rattle, constructed from a lattice of beads that is strung like a net over a hollowed-out gourd. The axatse plays a repeating part that is derived from the bell pattern.

For an example of this style of music, see YouTube video 'African 4: Ewe drumming'.

Melodic instruments

Balafon: this is a xylophone that is common to a number of west African countries. Like the djembe, it is thought to have originated among the Mandinke people during the early Mali Empire. The large wooden keys are strung over a frame, with a row of gourd resonators suspended underneath for amplification. The balafon is frequently tuned to a pentatonic scale, and tends to play fast ostinato-like patterns (similar to the kora). See for example YouTube video 'African 5: balafon'.

Kora: this is a west African harp that is primarily associated with the Mandinka people, and is common in Mali, The Gambia, Senegal, Guinea and Guinea-Bissau. Its body is made from one half of a large gourd that has been covered with cowhide; 21 strings run down from the long neck and over the bridge on the middle of the gourd. Tunings vary between regions but most use a heptatonic scale (F major, for example, is a very common tuning). Typically the thumbs play a bass ostinato while the index fingers play interweaving melodic lines (the other three fingers are used to hold the instrument upright).

Traditionally, west African kora players come from griot families, such as the Malian player Toumani Diabaté. Diabaté has played a pivotal role in introducing the kora to an international audience as a virtuosic instrument. You can watch him perform in YouTube video 'African 6: kora'.

Guitar and ngoni: the guitar was brought to Africa by the Portuguese as early as the 15th century, and has since become a staple instrument of African music, particularly within the popular genres that have developed during the last 100 years (such as Ghanaian highlife – see page 163). Guitar playing technique and repertoire in West Africa have been influenced by the music of older native instruments such as the kora and ngoni: a type of lute found throughout the region that is thought to be the ancestor of the American banjo. Bassekou Kouyate is probably the most famous exponent of the ngoni, and you can see him perform in YouTube video 'African 7: ngoni'.

MUSICAL GENRES

Drumming and polyrhythm

Drumming forms a major part of musical practice in west Africa. It accompanies a wide range of occasions – both formal and informal – and is frequently paired with dance. In rural areas in particular it can be strongly tied into the local religion: certain drums and drumming styles, for example, are considered to be sacred and capable of communicating with God.

Polyrhythm is also prevalent throughout west African percussive music (where two or more conflicting rhythms are heard together). Depending on the region or genre, this might involve anything from a couple of drums up to complex, multi-layered ensembles. An excellent example of west African polyrhythm (and drumming) is the music of the Anlo-Ewe, mentioned above on page 160.

Vocal music

Alongside drumming, it could be argued that vocal music is west Africa's other big musical genre. Singing pervades most types of music and is very much part of the fabric of society when it comes to both recreation and worship. In rural areas, choral singing is generally considered to be a community activity in which everyone can take part. Vocal music varies greatly in west Africa, from traditional songs in local languages to the Latin and English hymns of Christian worship.

Three common features of vocal music across sub-Saharan Africa are:

* Call and response, frequently between a soloist and chorus
* Homophonic textures
* Singing in close harmony.

The Tema Youth Choir from Ghana is one good example of a typical west African choir that mixes traditional songs with Christian choral music in their repertoire. The choir was founded in 2001 and has since become one of the country's top community choirs. YouTube video 'African 8: Tema Youth Choir' exemplifies the three characteristic features of vocal music listed above.

African choral music is becoming increasingly popular in the West. Various books of traditional songs exist, arranged for a variety of voices. Currently, quite a lot of this repertoire is South African based, possibly because of the global success of South African choirs such as Ladysmith Black Mambazo.

Highlife and hiplife

Highlife is a style of music that developed in Ghana in the early 1900s. It blended European dance styles, such as the foxtrot and waltz, with local west African dance rhythms and melodies. Other 'imported' genres such as Trinidadian calypso and Cuban son also had an influence on the genre. Highlife became very popular in selective dance halls and clubs around the coast, and with the elite ex-pat audience. One of the best-known performers of dance-based highlife is the trumpeter and bandleader E. T. Mensah – dubbed the 'king of highlife' – who was hugely popular throughout the 1940s–60s (see YouTube video 'African 9: Mensah').

After a few decades an offshoot of highlife emerged that was more guitar-driven and performed by smaller acoustic bands. One of the leading exponents of this type of highlife is Koo Nimo, who you can see perform in YouTube video 'African 10: Nimo'.

Hiplife, which fuses highlife with hip hop, emerged in the 1980s. It has become hugely popular and is currently more in vogue than highlife, which is today considered a little old-fashioned by younger audiences. Listen for example to the Ghanaian singer Obrafor (YouTube video 'African 11: Obrafor').

African blues, afrobeat and afropop

There is a growing consensus among academics that the origins of **the blues** lie in west Africa, rather than America. Some believe that characteristic features of early blues such as the call-and-response structure, melismatic vocal lines and nasal singing tone originated with the griots in Mali, brought to America by enslaved Africans.

Martin Scorsese's documentary *Feel Like Going Home* is a fascinating exploration into this theory, and provides an insightful comparison of American and African blues. A central feature of the film is a portrait of the legendary Malian blues guitarist and singer Ali Farka Toure. Nicknamed 'the African John Lee Hooker', his blues has a distinctly African flavour that has led him to international fame. You can watch him perform in YouTube video 'African 12: Toure'.

Fela Kuti was a highly influential west African musician who pioneered the genre of **afrobeat**. Born in Nigeria, he travelled to London in the 1950s where he studied music and developed a strong interest in jazz. The 1960s saw him fuse it with highlife and funk to create afrobeat. His music is highly political and he was championed both as a musician and a human-rights activist. Watch for example YouTube video 'African 13: Kuti'.

Salif Keita is one of the biggest stars of **afropop** (or African pop music). Born in Mali into a noble family, he was ostracised from his family and community partly because of his albinism (considered unlucky in Mandinka culture), and partly because music wasn't considered to be a suitable career for someone of his lineage. Despite this, he has had great international success with his music that fuses African rhythms, melodies and lyrics with Western pop instruments (see for example YouTube video 'African 14: Keita').

LISTENING EXAMPLE

George Darko is a celebrated Ghanaian highlife musician. He moved to Germany in the late 1970s, and was partly responsible for a new wave of highlife in the 1980s called 'burger highlife'. This added elements of funk and disco to the music. He has since moved back to Ghana and returned to a more traditional form of highlife.

Listen to the track 'Come to Africa' from the album *Highlife in the Air* (available on Spotify and iTunes), which is a joyful and upbeat celebration of Africa. It features the characteristic interlocking patterns and call and response that is typical of highlife (and west African music in general).

Introduction	
0:00	Electric guitar plays a 4-bar introductory riff accompanied by drum kit. Keyboards play sustained 'string' chords and countermelody. This song is in the key of B♭ major and is based upon alternating chords of B♭ and F.
0:08	A second electric guitar joins in, also playing a 4-bar ostinato. The interlocking guitar parts are typical of this style of music.

Chorus 1	
0:22	Bass guitar enters playing a 4-bar ostinato based around chords of B♭ and F. Interlocking guitar riffs, sustained keyboard chords and drums continue. Call and response between George Darko and a female backing chorus. *Woah Africa yeh (come to Africa)* *Mama Africa (come to Africa)* *Woah Africa yeh (come to Africa)* *I say you wanna come home? (come to Africa)*

Brass interlude 1	
0:38	Brass play a syncopated melody twice through.

Verse 1	
0:53	*You could be American, you could be a Russian* *You could be an Englishman, come to Africa* *You could be a German, you could be a Japanese* *You could be a Frenchman, I say come to Africa* *Come friend you'll see, people will feel like you* *Come friend you'll see, we are happy people* *Africa is not too hot, peace and happiness* *Sunshine and moonlight, it's where it began*

Chorus 2	
1:25	*Woah, woah woah, yeh Africa (come to Africa)* *I say you're welcome to Ghana yeh (come to Africa)* *Woah you're welcome Nigeria (come to Africa)* *I say you're welcome to Togo yeh (come to Africa)* *And now you're welcome Zimbabwe (come to Africa)* *I say you're welcome Cameroon yeh (come to Africa)* *And now you're welcome Côte d'Ivoire (come to Africa)*

Brass interlude 2	
1:53	Brass melody repeated twice.

Verse 2	
2:09	*If you come from Canada, if you come from Trinidad* *If you come from Barbados, come to Africa* *If you come from Portugal, if you come from Italy* *If you come from Australia, come to Africa* *Come friend you'll see, the land of rich culture* *Come friend you'll hear, African music through the air* *If you feel like dancing, come to Africa* *Highlife music, juju music, bakusa music and afrobeat* *Highlife music, soukous music, Africa, it's where it all began*

Chorus 3	
2:55	*Woah, woah woah, yeh Africa (come to Africa)* *I say you're welcome Mozambique (come to Africa)* *And now you're welcome Liberia (come to Africa)* *Woah you're welcome to Gabon yeh (come to Africa)* *And now you're welcome Senegal (come to Africa)* *I say you're welcome to Gambia yeh (come to Africa)* *And now you're welcome Morroco (come to Africa)* *I say you're welcome Tunisia yeh (come to Africa)* *And now you're welcome Soweto (come to Africa)*

Instrumental	
3:32	Balafon (on electric keyboard) plays a 4-bar ostinato. Electric guitars introduce two new descending riffs. Bass guitar deviates from its standard bass line.

Brass interlude 3	
4:13	Brass melody repeated twice; rest of the band return to their earlier parts.

Verse 3	
4:28	*Keep a smile on your face, Africa is not too hot* *Come on and take a friend, come to Africa* *You could be a Muslim, you could be a Christian* *You could be a Bulbisasi, come to Africa* *Come friend you'll see, our brothers and sisters* *All over the world, they wanna come home* *Come friend you'll see, the land of Shaka Zulu* *Haile Selassie and Kwame Nkrumah* *Nelson Mandela, struggling for freedom* *Total liberation, for our people* *God bless Africa, Mama Africa* *God bless Africa and all her people* *God bless Africa, Mama Africa* *God bless Africa and all her people* *Woah, woah woah, yeh Africa (come to Africa)*

Brass interlude 4	
5:32	Brass introduce a new 4-bar melody, which is repeated twice. Drums add tom-tom stabs.

Chorus 4	
5:47	*Woah you're welcome to Guinea yeh (come to Africa)* *And now you're welcome to Mali (come to Africa)* *I say you're welcome Sierra Leone yeh (come to Africa)* *And now you're welcome to Zambia (come to Africa)*

Brass interlude 5	
6:02	Brass repeat the new melody.
Chorus 5	
6:17	*Woah you're welcome to Kenya yeh (come to Africa)* *And now you're welcome Soweto (come to Africa)* *I say you're welcome Burkina yeh (come to Africa)* *Woah you're welcome to Ghana (come to Africa)*
6:32	Brass repeat the new melody until the song fades out.

After listening to *Come to Africa*, you could test your students' understanding of the song with these questions:

1. The guitar plays a riff in the introduction that lasts for four bars. Which two bars in this riff sound exactly the same? (The first and third bars)
2. How many times does the guitar play this riff before the singer enters? (Three)
3. The vocals in the chorus are an example of 'call and response'. What does this mean? (One phrase (the 'call') is answered by another (the 'response'). In African music, the call is usually sung by a soloist and the response by a chorus)
4. How would you describe the mood of the song? How is this mood created? (Happy/upbeat. Created by the major key; diatonic harmony; fairly fast tempo; strong drum beat; lively syncopated rhythms; upbeat lyrics)
5. In which chorus does the singer mention the country of Zimbabwe? (The second chorus)
6. Highlife music is a blend of west African and Western musical features. What 'Western' instruments can you hear in this song? (Drum kit; electric guitar; bass guitar; keyboards)
7. There are five main brass interludes in this song (the first starts at 0:38). Do the brass play the same tune in each one? If not, when does the tune change? (The tune changes in the third and fourth interludes. The first two interludes are the same; the fifth interlude repeats the tune from the fourth one)
8. How does the song end? (It fades out as the brass repeat their melody from the fourth and fifth interludes)
9. The song is inviting the listener to the continent of Africa, and the lyrics list numerous African countries. Choose six of these and find them on a map of Africa. Write down which part of Africa they are located in (i.e. north, east, south or west) and the capital city of each one.

PERFORMING

We mentioned the Anlo-Ewe drumming earlier on page 160 as a typical example of west African polyrhythm. The score for the traditional piece *Atsia* is provided on the book website. Although intended for a set of Ewe drums, this piece can effectively be recreated using any drums available. Here are a few pointers for performing this piece:

* All of the parts can be simplified according to the ability of your students. In this situation, making music is more important than worrying about authenticity!
* You can replace the gankogui with a Brazilian agogo or any other type of bell. Ideally the gankogui player should be able to create a 'high' and 'low' sound with their bell: the 'low' sound is used to indicate the start of each bar and so needs to be clearly heard.
* The axastse can be replaced with any type of shaker. This should be played by moving it up and down between the palm and the knee (see YouTube video 'African 7: Ewe drumming'). There should be more of these in the ensemble than any other instrument.
* The sogo part is for a drum played with two sticks, and should be the lowest-pitched drum. There are two types of stroke: an 'open' tone (where you hit the drum normally) and a 'push' tone (where the stick pushes against the skin so it doesn't ring, producing a duller sound). The sogo, kidi and kaganu can all be replaced by hand drums, perhaps using an open slap tone at the edge and a flat-handed dull tone in the centre.
* The kidi should be the medium-pitched drum, and is likewise played with sticks to create open and push tones.
* The kaganu is the highest-pitched drum, also played with sticks. In this piece it only plays open tones.
* A call-and-response song has been added to the score which perhaps half of your class can sing, while the other half play percussion.

It is common for Ewe drumming to be performed in very lengthy sessions that last for many hours. This often happens at celebrations, ceremonies and funerals. The community take turns to play the supporting drums, bell and rattles, constantly substituting parts as the day goes on. In keeping with this, you may want to encourage your students to learn all of the parts, teaching each part to the whole class as body percussion before handing out any instruments.

COMPOSING

Drumming piece

Your students could use the piece *Atsia* as a template for composing their own drumming piece. They may want to follow the steps below:

1. Compose a piece for five different instruments: bell, shaker, and three different-pitched drums.
2. Compose a 1 or 2-bar rhythm for each instrument that will be repeated throughout the piece. Remember that each instrument is essentially capable of producing two different pitches or tones ('high' and 'low' for the bell, 'open' and 'push' for the drums, and 'knee' and 'hand' for the shaker). The rhythms need to interlock together nicely when they are all played together!
3. Compose a short call-and-response song to accompany the drumming.

Your students could add in drum breaks or contrasting sections to expand the piece.

Highlife song

Having listened to George Darko's *Come to Africa* (and other examples of highlife music), your students could then write their own song in a highlife style, using the following pointers:

1. Compose a simple 4-bar riff in a major key, which can be played on guitar or another suitable melody instrument.
2. Compose a second riff that interlocks with the first. To make this easier, you could just play the first riff a 3rd or 6th lower, and then find small ways to vary it slightly.
3. Compose a 4-bar bass line that makes the music sound very dance-like, which should only be based on the primary chords (I, IV and V). This can then repeat throughout the rest of the song.
4. Compose a 1-bar rattle rhythm that can be repeated throughout the song.
5. Add a basic drum beat.
6. Write two verses and a chorus of lyrics based around the idea of having a good time. The chorus melody should have a call-and-response structure.

7. Compose melodies for the verse and chorus, based around your bass-line chords. The melody for either doesn't need to be too adventurous, but it should be catchy!
8. Compose a short instrumental interlude. This could have the same accompaniment as the rest of the song, which means you just need to compose a new 4-bar melody (perhaps to be played on brass instruments?).

To extend this, students could compose an introduction to the song and/or create a longer instrumental section.

CROSS-CURRICULAR LINKS

Dance link: in west Africa, music is strongly linked to dance which, in rural areas in particular, is very much a community activity. Of course 'African dance', like 'African music', is a huge generalisation, but on the whole it is lively, fun and easy to learn. There are various organisations in the UK that provide African dance workshops; could your students learn an African dance to accompany a drumming performance of *Atsia*? (Although from south rather than west Africa, the unique style of gumboot dancing is also well worth exploring, which combines dance with body percussion.)

Art link: Africa has a rich heritage of visual arts. As well as the more well-known traditional masks, carvings, paintings and textiles, there is also a vibrant contemporary art scene. Your students could explore the art of the ethnic groups whose music you have already studied, such as the weaving of the Ewe people, and the sculpture of the Yoruba people.

Geography link: the environment in west Africa varies from arid desert in the north to lush tropical rainforest in the south. There is much that can be explored in terms of the region's environment and demography. Students could also learn about one of the biggest problems facing the population of west Africa: drought and famine. Why are people in west Africa so dependent on a good rainfall? When was the last major famine in west Africa? What can the rest of the world do to help?

RESOURCES

Due to its popularity in the West, there are a wide range of resources available on African music. The following are some of the most useful for the music teacher.

Workshops

There are probably more workshop providers in the UK for African drumming than for any other style of world music. Given this, you shouldn't find it too difficult to find a local organisation that could bring djembes and other African drums into your school for a drumming workshop. Options for buying your own djembes in the UK also abound, from companies such as Inspire-works, Knock on Wood and Soar Valley Music.

Books and CDs

There are a great number of djembe tutor books available, but most of these are aimed at the individual player rather than the ensemble leader. Four books that should prove useful for music teachers are:

* *Music in West Africa* by Ruth M. Stone (Oxford University Press, 2004): a book that provides a good overview of west African music, accompanied by a CD.
* *Teach & Play African Drumming* by Mike Simpson (Rhinegold Education, 2012): a book of six African pieces designed for school use, accompanied by a DVD.
* *African Drumming Workshop: Kpatsa from Ghana* and *African Drumming Workshop: Ageshe from Ghana* by Trevor Wiggins (Rainbow Discs, 2007): two ebooks that break down individual drumming pieces and show you how to teach them to a class.

If you are looking for good compilation CDs that act as a taster to African music, try the record label Putumayo (who produce CDs such as *African Playground*, which is accompanied by a free teaching guide on their website), or the 'Rough Guide' CDs (*The Rough Guide to Highlife, The Rough Guide to Mali,* etc.).

The computer program 'West African drumming' from Wells Music Academy is also worth a mention (www.academy.wellscathedralschool.org/): this is a free downloadable program that allows you to take part in a 'virtual' Ewe drumming ensemble and also includes a composing project.